YOU MATTER

Fully Seen, Fully Known, and Fully Loved

YOU MATTER

Fully Seen, Fully Known, and Fully Loved

True Stories and Devotions of Bravery and Courage to Strengthen Your Faith Journey

DeAnna D. Cavenah

with Shirley Fontenot, Victoria Bennett, Jaime Hebert, Angela Hardy, Kathy Boykin, Lacy Saucier, Candace Havard, Marlena Carlin, Stefanee Tolbert, Catherine Deere, Bethany Taylor, Angela Broussard, Natalie Fitkin, Shanyetta Hypolite, Connie Book, Toni Petrofes, Rena Beadle, Hadley Martin, Izabel Buxton, Denise LeDoux Leiato, and Melissa Richard,

Buy the Book, Help a Family

A portion of the proceeds of this book will go to support Lighthouse Ministries, Inc. a Non-Profit Child Residential Home located in Reeves, LA that houses unwed mothers and their children. Your support helps provide a safe haven for these young mothers and their babies, giving them a chance to start fresh and build a better future for themselves and their children.

Additionally, there may be times other Non-Profit Organizations that house women of domestic violence, abuse and addictions will be highlighted. By supporting this book, you are also contributing to the safety, recovery, and empowerment of women in need. Your generosity helps provide shelter, resources, and hope to those who are rebuilding their lives.

Dedication

I dedicate *You Matter* to my mother, Shirley Ann Fontenot. I am and will always be grateful to my mom for raising me to have the fear and reference for not only the Lord but the House of the Lord. I am thankful to have a mother that refused to let hell have me. During the time I was away from the Lord at a young age, she remained in a position of prayer literally fighting the demonic realm demanding that it loose its hold on me as I was choosing a lifestyle that was destroying me. Today I am the fruit of her prayers and proud to be called her daughter. Together we have seen healing and restoration of our relationship and in our individual lives.

Between these pages, you will find her story. A story of bravery that will not only amaze you but will move you to compassion knowing that no matter what life throws at you, You Matter, and you can overcome. You can rise up and break generational curses and make better choices for yourself and your family. You already have on the inside what you need to succeed. You are fearfully and wonderfully made, with much potential and purpose. You are fully known and deeply loved by your Heavenly Father.

Thank you, Mom, for choosing a better life for yourself and your children. Thank you for the way you raised us and took care of all of our needs. I'm so honored for you to be a part of this project.

Acknowledgments

To all the brave women who took the time to tell their stories through the pages of this project, I say "Thank You!" Without you, this project could have never become a reality. Thank you for your BIG obedient yes! When you said yes to me, you were saying yes to the Lord. Your stories and devotions have the opportunity to encourage and transform the lives of many women. It is a seed that will continue to reap a great harvest. Thank you for sharing your lives with the world. Remember, "You Matter" to me.

To my publisher, Katelyn Silva, thank you for your dedication and patience while I acted like a sloth. It took me a while, but I finally got moving. I'm forever grateful to you for helping me get these stories into the hands of my readers.

"Here's another way to put it: You're here to be light, bringing out the God-colors in the world. God is not a secret to be kept. We're going public with this, as public as a city on a hill. If I make you light-bearers, you don't think I'm going to hide you under a bucket, do you? I'm putting you on a light stand. Now that I've put you there on a hilltop, on a light stand—shine! Keep open house; be generous with your lives. By opening up to others, you'll prompt people to open up with God, this generous Father in heaven."
Matthew 5:14-16 MSG

Table of Contents

Preface

I couldn't wait to get this book into your hands to tell you that YOU MATTER! Not only do you matter to me, but you are not alone in your struggle. God knows you, God sees you, and God fully loves you.

Most people know this, but what about the people we live with every day of our lives? Sometimes we can buy the lie that we don't matter. I have found out that most people carry around such brokenness that they themselves find it hard to show kindness or compassion. They also tend to view the world from their tainted perspective or what they are currently going through.

Let's get something straight from the beginning; we all go through things and life can knock all of us down at times.

Years ago I read an article that claimed that when you give a friend or even someone you may not know a pinwheel, you are telling that person, "You Matter." Not only are you saying, "You matter," but, "You Matter to Me!" That truly impacted me and changed the way I viewed a pinwheel. In life, it's essential to remind those we care about just how significant they are. Sometimes, the simplest of gestures can have the most profound impact on a person's life. This seemingly whimsical and childlike object carries with it a depth of symbolism and meaning that can convey your heartfelt appreciation and acknowledge their importance in your life. In our fast-paced world, it's easy to overlook the small gestures that can make a big difference.

The pinwheel has a rich history and cultural significance. In various cultures, such as China, it is considered a symbol of good fortune and positive energy. In Western societies, they evoke memories of carefree childhood days, symbolizing innocence and the simple pleasures of life.

Even from childhood I have always enjoyed a pinwheel but never knew the significance other than it being a fun toy.

A pinwheel, with its vibrant colors and playful spinning, is more than just a toy. It symbolizes joy, vitality, and the cycles of life. As it spins, it reflects the ups and downs, the shared laughter, and the unspoken support that form the foundation of a friendship.

The act of giving is a powerful way to show someone they matter. When you present your friend with a pinwheel, you are not just giving them an object but also sharing a piece of your heart. This gesture signifies that you have thought about them, that you recognize and appreciate their presence in your life, and that you are committed to nurturing and celebrating your friendship.

Letting someone know they matter is an essential part of nurturing and sustaining relationships. So, the next time you wish to let someone know they matter, consider the humble pinwheel—a gift that spins with fun, joy, love, and appreciation.

Introduction

To every woman reading this, know that you are cherished and valued. Your story with all its highs and lows is a beautiful tapestry woven with threads of grace and resilience. You matter, and your journey is important. Embrace it, share it, and let it shine brightly for others to see. Your voice has power, your experiences have meaning, and your presence is a blessing to this world.

You are not alone. You are loved. You matter.

Your life matters, and you are a vital part of the grand tapestry of existence. Each moment of joy, every challenge you overcome, and every step you take is significant. Regardless of the trials you face, your resilience and courage inspire those around you. Your presence brings light and love to the world, and you have an undeniable impact on the lives you touch.

Remember to nurture your soul, take care of your heart, and honor your journey. Embrace the uniqueness of your path and the lessons it brings. Stand tall in your truth, and let your life be a testament to the power of faith, hope, and love.

To understand why you matter, it is essential to recognize your own self-worth. Self-worth is the deep-seated belief that you are valuable simply for being who you are. It is not contingent upon external achievements, accolades, or even the approval of others. Embracing self-worth means acknowledging and recognizing that your presence in this world is significant. You are uniquely created by the Creator of the Universe, your Heavenly Father.

Building self-worth is a lifelong journey that begins with self-compassion. It involves treating yourself with kindness and understanding, especially during moments of failure or self-doubt. Practicing self-compassion fosters resilience and helps you bounce back from setbacks, seeing them as opportunities for growth rather than as reflections of your worth.

Another key component of self-worth is self-acceptance. This means embracing all facets of your identity, including your strengths and imperfections. Self-acceptance allows you to live authentically and to pursue your passions and goals without the burden of unrealistic expectations.

When you recognize your self-worth, it transforms the way you interact with the world. You become more confident in your abilities and more willing to take risks and pursue your dreams. This confidence radiates outward, positively influencing your relationships and inspiring others to recognize their own value.

Every person's story is a mosaic of experiences, emotions, and lessons learned. Your story is unique, and it matters because it shapes who you are and how you perceive the world.

Your story has the potential to impact others in ways you may never fully realize. By sharing your journey, you can inspire, motivate, and offer hope to those who may be navigating similar challenges. Your story can serve as a beacon of light, guiding others through their own dark moments and helping them to find strength and resilience.

The ripple effect of your story extends far beyond your immediate circle. Many people carry silent burdens, feeling isolated and misunderstood. By sharing your story, you break the silence and create space for others to share their own experiences. This act of vulnerability can bring much freedom and can help to dismantle the stigma surrounding various issues, such as mental health, addiction, and trauma.

Embracing your journey means recognizing that every experience, both positive and negative, has shaped you into the person you are today. It involves finding meaning in your struggles and celebrating your successes. By embracing your journey, you honor your resilience and acknowledge the growth that has come from your experiences.

Finding meaning in your struggles does not mean minimizing or dismissing the pain you have endured. Instead, it involves seeing your challenges as opportunities for growth and transformation. Every obstacle you overcome strengthens your character and equips you for the future. It is a testament of your perseverance and determination

Remember, your presence in this world is significant, and your story has the power to bring hope, healing, and transformation. Embrace your journey, for it is uniquely yours, and it matters deeply. "You Matter!"

I Believe in You,

DeAnna

A person without
Self-Control is like a
city with broken
down walls.
~Proverbs 25:28~

Self-Control

DeAnna D. Cavenah

God is close to the brokenhearted!

"If your heart is broken, you'll find God right there; if you're kicked in the gut, he'll help you catch your breath." ~
Psalms 34:18 MSG

In 2022, I became a first-time author, and all I can say is, "The Lord has done it again." From time to time He will use my devotional, "Not Defined By The Struggle" to minister to me. In the particular devotion, "God is close to the brokenhearted" it speaks of a physical death, but there are many other types of death that a person can walk through: the death of a dream, death of a friendship, death of a marriage, etc.

Have you ever thought about this one—death to SELF!

"But the fruit of the Spirit [the result of His presence within us] is love [unselfish concern for others], joy, [inner] peace, patience [not the ability to wait, but how we act while waiting], kindness, goodness, faithfulness, gentleness, self-control." ~ Galatians 5:22-23 AMP

Ok, so I don't know about you but when I read these verses, especially on mornings like this, I really don't like that last fruit, ughhh, SELF-CONTROL!

At first, these two verses from Psalms and Galatians seem like they have nothing in common and then again, they have everything in common.

You see, the Lord already knew what I would face when I woke up and he already knew the hand/person by which it would come. He already knew that I would want to take matters into my own hands and defend myself or express my feelings, and how I felt kicked in the gut.

Don't you just hate when you type out that social media post because you need to set the record straight and then you feel that gentle nudge to delete it? So then you pick up your phone and record a 10-minute message to send them and then you hear that gentle whisper, "Delete that." Am I in this struggle alone or have you ever experienced this too?

No matter how saved we are, I believe we can all be guilty of it from time to time. This is called "Death to Self", dying to your flesh. I went on a missions trip to another country and literally smelled human flesh burning and there is no pretty way to say it: "It stinks." In our flesh dwells no good thing. My flesh thinks Self-Control stinks, but when my spirit gets engaged with it it's such a beautiful smell unto the Lord; because when we use Self-Control we are surrendering.

My friend, whatever you woke up facing that has come to steal your peace, distract you, get you off track, or kick you in the gut, know that the Lord has already seen it and He wants you to run to Him with it.

Going back to the verse we started with in Psalms, let's look at what the verse before says, "Yet when holy lovers of God cry out to him with all their hearts, the Lord will hear them and come to rescue them from all their troubles." ~ Psalms 34:17 TPT

See? You don't have to strive and perform Self-Control on your own. You can just take everything to the Lord and let Him do the work and bear the fruit in you.

You've got this! Go ahead and flip the script!

Just keep your focus on Him and allow the fruit of the Spirit, Self-Control, to continually be developed in your life. He has you covered; let Him handle your concerns. Remember You Matter and What happens to you Matters to God.

Reflection Questions:

The Fruit of the Spirit has to be developed in our lives. Which fruit do you struggle with most?

_____

When is the last time that you had to exercise Self-Control?

_____

_____

_____

_____

How did that situation turn out?

_____

_____

_____

_____

_____

Life isn't always fair. It's not always about what happens to us but rather in us. Is there a situation or person you need to surrender to the Lord? If so, pray this prayer:

Dear Lord,

Thank you for your unwavering love and guidance. Help me to cultivate the fruit of self-control in my life. When I am faced with challenges that test my resolve, grant me the strength to remain steadfast in You. Teach me to surrender my worries and fears into Your hands, trusting in Your divine plan and perfect timing. May I find peace in Your presence and the courage to let go of what I cannot control. Guide my heart and mind towards Your will, and let Your wisdom be my anchor. In Jesus' name, Amen.

<u>**Worship Encounter:**</u>

"Selah III Fruits of the Spirit" by Hillsong Young and Free

"Defender" by Rita Springer

"I Surrender" by Hillsong

God will make a way,
where there seems
to be no way.
He works in ways we
cannot see.
~Don Moen~

Fully Seen, Fully Known, and Fully Loved by God

Shirley Fontenot

Even when I didn't know the Lord, He not only knew me but saw exactly where I was and what I was going through. After all these years I'm still in awe of how His love carried me through some of the darkest times of my life.

I was born and grew up in the city of Detroit, Michigan, and I grew up in a very dysfunctional home. My mother, who was an alcoholic, left my brother and I alone when I was only four years old to live with my father. She told us that she was coming back to get us, but those were just empty words. She never did. When she married my dad she had a son, Gene, from a previous relationship. When she got pregnant with my brother, Charlie, she and my dad dropped Gene off in Birmingham, Alabama at my grandmother's house. She told my grandmother she would go back to pick him up, but she never did. He was only four years old as well. She did to him exactly what she did to me and my brother.

I know now that she was a broken, unhealed woman, incapable of raising any of us due to her addiction and inability to even love or care for herself. She remained in Detroit where she was a cook in many different restaurants. She was a very good cook, but we never ate her food. Every once in a while we would visit her. She had the ability to come visit us every Saturday. I would wait by the window, hoping she would come, but she would never show up. I guess it wasn't until I had my own son, John, at the age of 18 that I realized she was never going to come back.

I wish I could say I was better off living with my dad but unfortunately, that was not my reality. My dad not only had a drinking problem, but a woman problem too. My dad would often tell me that I was just like my mother.

I really don't have any pleasant memories of my childhood. I was never allowed to be involved in any activities at school. My dad wouldn't even allow us to do homework. No one was ever allowed to come into our home, and we weren't allowed to go anywhere.

Anytime he would take my brother and me places, he would always leave us in the car, sometimes for hours. Even when he was at a relative's home. My dad would have women in and out of our lives. I remember one of those women very well, Goldie. She would come and go but lived with us most of the time. She never cooked; she smoked and drank; that's about it.

Goldie did not like me, which was obvious by the lies she would tell about me. What I didn't know at the time was that she was jealous of me, and I guess she thought I was in the way of her relationship with my dad. I remember one time she told a lie about me, and my dad came in my room and beat me. I was used to seeing him beat women, but I never thought that I would become one of his victims. Sometimes it would get so bad at home that I would just put a comb in my pocket and leave for days. Usually, the police would have to pick me up and take me to juvenile detention.

Goldie convinced my dad that I was so bad I needed to go to a boarding school, so that's where he sent me. My dad was an interior decorator and painter by trade. He had done some work at a Catholic Reform School and wanted me to go there. I didn't stay there very long though because I wouldn't follow their rules. Although I love fish now, I hated it then and refused to eat it. I would often get written up for that.

After leaving there, I had to go to another Reform School which was very strict. The whole time I stayed there I never took a shower or a bath because the girls wanted to have their way with you. I ran away from there and hid in a barn. I finally realized that I couldn't stay in that barn forever and decided to go live on the streets.

I definitely know that the Lord was protecting me because three boys picked me up in their car and brought me out into the country. They dropped me off at a little church and told me that I would be safe there and that they would come back and pick me up. They could have abused me out there, but they didn't; they were never disrespectful in any way. They did come back for me and brought me back to Detroit, to my mother's home. I'm not sure why I went there or even thought she could help me because she had never helped me before. I was sitting on her front porch when a lady told me that my mother no longer lived there. I had no choice but to go back to my dad's.

The next morning he and Goldie brought me to live with Goldie's mother in Kentucky. She was a lot like Goldie. I ended up staying there for the summer, and then I went back to my dad's.

Very shortly after, I turned 18 and moved to Birmingham, Michigan to live with some people I worked for. One day I called a girl I went to school with to come pick me up; I met a guy who was friends with her boyfriend. I started seeing him on the weekends and he appeared to be a really nice guy. After seeing him for a while he wanted to get married, so we did. Very shortly afterward, I realized he was not all he had appeared to be. He had a big problem with other women. I got pregnant immediately after we married, and he did not want children. If we were out he wouldn't even speak to me. He acted like he didn't even know me. He stopped coming home when he got off work on Friday and was gone all weekend.

I remember it was wintertime; I had finally had enough of being treated that way and moved out. I got a room and found a job at a factory. His mother told me that she knew of a good doctor I could go to, and she wrote his name and address on a matchbox for me. I met a friend and she informed me that the doctor was an abortionist. When they found out I had not gone to the doctor, my husband and his mother thought they would trick me.

I had Johnny, and the next morning the nurse asked what my husband thought about the baby. I told her he didn't know. So the nurse called him, and he and his mother came to the hospital to see us. He seemed happy and even asked if we could give him Melvin as his middle name and I agreed. The following morning the nurse told me that she had met with the adoptive family, and they were real nice. I told her that my baby was not up for adoption. Once again my husband and his mother had thought they would pull something over on me.

When I had my son, I'm not sure why, but again I thought my mother could help me, even though she never helped me before. She told me she could help take care of him while I worked. So I got an apartment and she started staying with me. The first night I woke up and went into the front room and she was on the couch drunk with a man. I made him leave. She told me that she threw the whiskey bottle away; we had a thing called a dumbbell—a chute from the pantry to the basement to put trash in. I saw she had actually put the whiskey bottle on the side of it, so I just slipped it in.

Later, she wanted to know where the whiskey was, I said, "Well you told me you threw it." So there was a scene with her. I told her to get out and that I didn't ever want to see her again. And I didn't see her again, until she went into the hospital. Every time she went to the hospital, who did they call? Me, every time one of her boyfriends broke her arm or something else, they'd always call me, and it was always around Christmas time.

Let me back up a little from that hospital call.

I was having a really hard time, I had come to the end of my rope and couldn't find anyone to help me with taking care of my baby. I only made $1.00 an hour in the factory and that's exactly what babysitters charged. I went to Newberry's, a local dime store, to purchase some clothes for my baby so that I could give him away. I didn't want to give up my baby, I wanted to keep him, but I saw no way out of that situation. My dad had always told me that when times got hard enough, I would give him up. I didn't want my dad's words to be true, I was not like my mother, but it was so hard and I thought I had no other choice but to give him up.

As I looked for baby clothes a woman began to talk to me. She was looking for baby clothes too as a gift for someone else. She told me that she was never able to have children of her own. I didn't realize it at the moment, but this woman was sent straight from God. I was going to give Johnny to her. As I began to talk with her, she told me she would go home and talk with her husband about taking care of Johnny for me. She called me the next day and agreed to take him.

At that point, Ann became family for me and Johnny. She and her husband ended up having to move from where they lived because their apartment complex did not allow children. After finding another apartment in order to keep him, it was only months later that they moved from where we lived in Detroit, Michigan to Kinder, Louisiana. They offered to take me and Johnny with them—he was 11 months old at the time. I agreed to go with them, and it was the best move I have ever made in my life. Ann took care of Johnny for me while I worked at a local diner in Kinder called Bolos and that's where I met and later married my husband, Ermin.

So fast forward, when I got the call about my mother being in the hospital, I was living in Louisiana and pregnant with my second child. They had found my mom on the street, alive but unconscious in the snow. She was brought to the hospital and they had to do fingerprints. They found out she was from Alabama, and from that traced her back to Michigan. My husband and I were in a hard time financially, but we went and borrowed money from a finance company. I took Johnny, who was then four years old, and rode the bus to Michigan. Johnny stayed with my dad while I stayed at the hospital with my mom for three days.

I was sitting with my mother on the third day and I looked over and noticed she had died. I had been with several people when they died, so I knew the look. She was conscious the day before and she had looked like she was alert, but when I went into the room she didn't know me from a nurse. She never talked to me but when my dad came in the room she called him by name and asked him if he would bring her up to the farm. My dad had bought a farm in Marlette—about 70 miles from Detroit—after I had moved out. That's actually where Johnny was born.

I went to tell the nurse she had died, and the nurse said she couldn't have passed because she had just been in there to check on her. She went in and confirmed my mom had indeed passed away. They wanted to know who would be taking care of her body. Her first husband, Jack, who I had never seen before, showed up, but he said he could not do anything. So I called my husband, and he went back to another finance company and sent money to me so I could bury her. After I took care of those arrangements, Johnny and I took a bus back to Kinder, Louisiana.

Before my second child, Karen, was born my dad would come to Kinder to try to get me to move back to Michigan with him. But the day came when my dad not only moved to Kinder, but moved in with us. I was able to forgive him for all that I went through as a child and all of the things I carried into adulthood, but it was only because of the relationship I had developed with the Lord. My dad was able to see me raise all four of my children. I know it was the Lord that allowed him to see that I was not like my mother. He lived with us until he passed away in May of 1975.

I didn't know God at the time I moved to Louisiana, but I'm so glad that He knew me. He not only knew me, but He saw me in my desperation and raised up a woman to reach out to me and be the light in my dark place. God used Ann to rescue me and to give me and my baby a home in the natural. We became best friends, and our families remained in each other's lives until she passed away in 1991. She gave me a natural home, but years later before she passed, Ann gave her life to the Lord and now she has an eternal home.

Reflection Questions:

Have you ever felt that your back was against a wall and you saw no way out? Explain:

_____

_____

_____

_____

_____

How did you see God move for you in that situation?

_____

_____

_____

_____

_____

_____

Maybe you find yourself in a difficult season of your life right now. If that is you, pray this prayer today and believe that God is for you and not against you. Begin to see this situation turning around for your good.

Heavenly Father,

I am grateful that You know me, that You see me in every moment of my life and love me completely. No matter what challenges I face, I find comfort in knowing that Your presence surrounds me.

In times when it feels like there is no way out and my back is against the wall, I ask for Your divine intervention. Lord, please give me the strength and courage to endure the challenges I may face and the hope to believe brighter days are ahead.

Wrap me in Your comforting embrace and remind me that I am never alone. Fill my heart with Your peace and my mind with clarity to see the path You have set before me. Help me to trust in Your infinite wisdom and love, knowing that You have plans to prosper me and not to harm me.

Thank You, Lord, for hearing my prayer and for being my refuge and strength in times of trouble. Amen.

Deeper Truth:

Isaiah 43:1-4 (MSG),
Jeremiah 29:11 (NLT),
Romans 8:28 (AMP),
Genesis 50:20 (NLT)

Worship Encounter:

"Known" by Tauren Wells
"You Made a Way" by Jon Reddick
"You Know My Name" by Tasha Cobbs Leonard

Only God can turn a mess
into a message,
A test into a testimony,
A trial into a triumph,
A victim into a victor.
~Fern Berstein~

Don't Let the Mess Fool You
Victoria Bennett

Be still, be calm, see and understand I am the True God. –
Psalms 46:10 – Voice Translation

On my way to New Mexico, my husband spotted LOTS of cattle. Like ants on a kicked mound, they covered the hills! My spirit leaped thinking, "The Lord promises the cattle on 1,000 hills!" My excitement ended quickly as the aroma of manure filled the vehicle. EWW! I told him, "I don't know if I want the cattle on 1,000 hills with all that mess!" Now grieved, I pondered how we often allow the "mess" to stop us from God's promise. When things are not going smoothly or not going how we think they should, we often abort the promise prematurely.

One of the messiest seasons of my life was walking through divorce. Shame, guilt, rejection, abandonment, fear, uncertainty—just to name a few emotions—swirled through my mind as I signed those documents. The chaos and torment were exhausting, at best. I fell on my face, eyes swollen and full of tears, and lamented before the Father. I cried and begged for Him to take me out of my misery! After this pity party, lying on the floor helpless, a still, small voice said, "I'm with you wherever you go. I will never leave or forsake you. Be strong and courageous!"

I'd be lying if I said it was completely smooth for me after this encounter with God. It was not! However, I knew I could make it through the "mess" ahead to the promise. Often, we must go through the "mess" so God can do something inside of us. I walked through lots of acknowledging pain and trauma to receive healing. There were also messy areas within me that needed purging.

I grew more in these four years than in my entire life. I surrounded myself with mature women of faith to encourage me and share wisdom. I stayed connected to my home church and to the vine, my God, my life source for everything. God brought my current husband into my life, and this also was covered in mess. Boy, am I glad I didn't skip him because of the" mess"! I would have missed my promised land. God is so faithful!

I look back and see God's paintbrush as He painted a masterpiece in my life through the "mess"! Be encouraged that no matter the "mess" you face, God has a promise on the other side. Hold His hand tight and keep pressing forward. He promises a victory!

Reflection Questions:

What has God promised me that I am still waiting to see come to pass?

_____

_____

What area in my life do I currently feel is a "mess"?

_____

_____

Take a moment and allow the Holy Spirit to speak to you and show you how your mess is a part of the promise God has made you. Write what Jesus would tell you about the "mess" you find yourself in.

_____

_____

_____

<u>Worship Encounter:</u>

"Take It All Back"

by Tauren Wells

"Jireh" by Maverick City

"Spirit Lead Me" by Michael Ketterer and Influence

Be still and KNOW
that I am God
Psalm 46:10

Be Still

Jaime Hebert

There have been many times in my life when I have been seeking answers or needing a breakthrough. In those moments I have felt helpless or even desperate awaiting God's response. Sometimes I have seen a swift shift but in most instances, His response has been a soft "Be Still". In my desperation, I picture myself as a toddler at the feet of my father tugging at his pants crying out for his immediate attention. I don't know what the answer needs to be. I just know I want it now.

You see I was a 16-year-old high-school dropout, pregnant without much hope for a bright future. I faced rejection and insecurities that ran deep, so I continued to search for love in all the wrong places. The enemy truly had a plan to destroy me, but God had a bigger plan.

By the age of 24, I was a single mother with six small children. It felt as if I could do nothing right; every man I thought would be my savior would use and abuse me. There was one thing I knew I could do: bring my kids to church. Lots of times those three hours at church were just a break for me, where I was surrounded by people I trusted. I thought I was beyond help and that there was no way to fix all my mistakes. I wore a mask and a smile to cover my personal traumas and feelings. I just kept getting up each day surviving and doing my best to create a stable and decent home for my kids.

Even though I was hiding and only sitting in the church chair for my kids, my God saw me and began to prove Himself to me in every area of my life. He pursued me and showed me how much He loved me and that I was not alone. As my relationship with my savior developed, the promises in His word came to life through my life.

You see God knew every mistake I would make before I ever made it. He planned great things for me and no matter how many obstacles my mistakes threw His way He never changed His mind. He chose me to parent each of my children and they were not mistakes; they were already part of His plan.

At 46 years old I am now the wife of an amazing husband. My six children have all grown into adults and I have three bonus children. Together my husband and I now have 16 amazing grandchildren. I am a successful businesswoman with a career I could have never imagined. We live a blessed life that feels like a dream.

If I could go back to the 16-year-old girl who was alone and hopeless I would tell her, "Remember to Be Still and Know that He is God."

Reflection:

Let's read the entire chapter of Psalm 46. Pay special attention to verses 5-6 and verse 10.

Psalm 46

¹ God is our refuge and strength,
an ever-present help in trouble.
² Therefore we will not fear, though the earth give way
and the mountains fall into the heart of the sea,
³ though its waters roar and foam
and the mountains quake with their surging.
⁴ There is a river whose streams make glad the city of God,
the holy place where the Most High dwells.
⁵ God is within her, she will not fall;
God will help her at break of day.
⁶ Nations are in uproar, kingdoms fall;
he lifts his voice, the earth melts.
⁷ The Lord Almighty is with us;
the God of Jacob is our fortress.
⁸ Come and see what the Lord has done,
the desolations he has brought on the earth.
⁹ He makes wars cease
to the ends of the earth.
He breaks the bow and shatters the spear;
he burns the shields with fire.
¹⁰ He says, "Be still, and know that I am God;
I will be exalted among the nations,
I will be exalted in the earth."
¹¹ The Lord Almighty is with us;
the God of Jacob is our fortress.

When was a time in your life when you learned to "Be Still and Know."

_____

_____

_____

_____

_____

_____

_____

_____

What is the Holy Spirit speaking to you now as you read these verses in Psalm 46?

_____

_____

_____

_____

_____

_____

_____

_____

_____

How can you integrate this into your habits moving forward?

_____

_____

_____

_____

_____

Worship Encounter:

"Be Still and Know" by CeCe Winans

"Goodness of God" by Bethel Music

"Be Still" by Steffany Gretzinger

Honesty is often very hard. The truth is often painful, but the freedom it can bring is worth the trying.
~Fred Rogers~

Truth Matters

DeAnna D. Cavenah

You matter, and because you matter, truth matters. I've always been told, and you have probably always heard, that real friends will tell you the truth. Can we be honest here? The truth isn't always easy; sometimes it's downright hard to hear. I'll take it a step further... it can also make you very angry at times.

All my life I have been in sales, from selling Avon, skin care, and real estate, to owning my own gift shop. It's always been a part of my DNA makeup. I think I get it from my daddy. At the age of 90, most days you can find him in his shop making swings, wooden cars, and trains to sell.

Last night, at the time of writing this, when I came home my husband proceeded to tell me that he went into our spare bedroom and basically was horrified by what he saw. "Deanna, what is all that stuff?" was his question. Boxes lined the walls, boxes were underneath the pool table, and piles of stuff were in the corners.

I started to plead my case, "That's all of my inventory for my booth." I rent a booth at a local vendors' market; remember, I love selling things.

He proceeded to tell me that I could not continue to clutter up the spare room because, "You can barely get around in there. Don't even think about playing pool, oh, did I mention, there is stuff piled on top of the pool table?"

I once again began to plead my case, "I'm an entrepreneur, it's in my DNA." And may I add, I wanted him to be proud of that fact. But here's the hard truth... I knew he was right.

"You're right!" Two little words that cause much pain when we have the strength to let them come out of our mouth.

Let me be honest, I didn't tell him that in the moment because in that moment, I was mad. There was a wrestling match going on inside of me between his words, my desires, and Holy Spirit's voice. Here's an even harder truth: I had spent two full days in that room the week prior, deep cleaning and decluttering. I was overwhelmed and stressed out because of all the time it was consuming.

Although I was cleaning out and organizing, I kept hearing that gentle voice telling me that this was keeping me from the rest that He intended for me. All this stuff was not only cluttering up the room but cluttering up my mind and my time. I had become burdened down with stuff! I had been holding on to things and accumulating more things for a "someday", and at the same time forfeiting my peace and rest.

God said He would give us the desires of our heart. Sometimes that comes by way of letting go of the things that have a grip on us. He wants us to be in His grip. He says, "My yoke is easy, and My burden is light." I realized in that moment that I hadn't been yoked up to Him but rather I was yoked up with stuff. I was carrying a heavy burden, but I was putting it on myself. I knew it was time for a new strategy, a new plan of action. Remember: you matter and your desires matter, but so does truth. Will you embrace it today and learn to rest in the knowledge of that freedom?

Ask the Lord to help you to be sensitive to His voice and receive the truth, even when it's hard. He wants to reveal it to you, even if it comes through a friend.

Reflections Questions:

Can you remember a time when someone told you a hard truth and you knew they were right? What was your response?

_____

_____

_____

Can you identify some things that you may be yoked up with that is causing unrest in this season?

_____

_____

_____

Look back over your answer in #2 and write out a prayer to the Lord asking Him to help you submit those things to Him so that you can be yoked up with Him and experience His Peace and His Rest.

_____

_____

_____

_____

_____

_____

Deeper Truth:
Matthew 11:29 (AMP)
Psalms 37:4 (AMP)
John 8:32 (TPT)

<u>**Worship Encounter:**</u>

"Easy" by Mercy Culture

"Make Room"

by Community Music

"Lord Send Revival" by

Hillsong Young and Free

Even the smallest
shift in perspective
can bring about the
greatest healing."
~Unknown~

Perspective Changes Things

Angela Hardy

Have you ever really thought about the word "perspective" and its true meaning?

It's all about a different point of view, a way of seeing the world, a new attitude. It's a perception, or discernment, insight, and wisdom. For example, all the Gospels are the same, but told in a different man's view, a different perspective. So, seeing things from a different perspective requires an open (mental) view. The word comes from a Latin root that means "look through" or "perceive from a new viewpoint."

And I needed one badly!

I lost my husband a few years ago and I must confess, I was initially very angry with God. We were strong, faithful Christians of 45+ years. Very faithful to church, very faithful to God. How could God let this happen? We did not deserve this, nor did we believe for anything other than complete healing. I was in shock because I just knew he'd be healed. My way!

I now realize as I reflect: it's truly a part of the mourning process to even think and be upset like that, but I was super angry and really afraid about those thoughts. But while in the process I could not understand God's reasoning for choosing to take my husband just three years after his retirement. They were our very best years together. It was a new journey we had been waiting for. And we were like newlyweds.

God's mercy stayed with me as the months went by and I'd hear certain phrases, testimonies, stories, etc. that would end up helping me make it through each day. Little by little things were melting my stony heart. Of course I wanted to be better and stronger in the Lord. And of course I wanted it to happen immediately. I didn't want to be an angry Christian! But no, it was such a slow process.

Then one day I heard a testimony from a young couple who lost their young infant baby to cancer. I mean I could not comprehend having a new, beautiful gift of God come into my life, and then be taken less than a year later. "What's the point, God? I'm sorry but I can NOT understand your ways."

Well, let me tell you, this couple amazed me and put me to shame. They testified that they were grateful to God for blessing their lives with this baby for even a short 10 months. For all the joy she brought to them and others in such a short time. And even though she was gone so soon, it was far better to have had her, than to never have brought her into their lives to love at all.

WHAT? How could they possibly, at the funeral of that precious new life, be so positive? I was still angry for them, and they were looking at her life in a whole new perspective. They were blessed by her presence, no matter how small.

God gave them to her for a purpose and she accomplished her purpose in life. I don't know what it was, and I don't know if they completely know. But what I do know is, hearing the story of baby Caroline blessed my life! And her parents blessed my life and many others through their testimony of her and this short, sweet life, so God did use her in many great ways.

Who's to say that one life can't bless as many or more hearts in such a short time, than another that He might use for years and years? God is in control, and He knows what it takes for whoever He needs, whenever and however. We are not to doubt Him at all. Can we question Him? Absolutely! But then, we must trust Him. Is it easy? Absolutely NOT. But it's a perspective that I had never imagined. And I wanted to gain it somehow. I knew it was a good thing.

My husband had seven heart attacks and God brought him through each and every one. We glorified God in all of them, and God gave us 23 more years together. Those last years were far greater than the first 25. We grew so close and more in love every year. Instead of wondering why God took him after things were getting better, I now often try to say, "Thank you, Father God, for all those extra years of beautiful love, growth, and togetherness. They were better than our first and I am so grateful to have had those years of memories with my very best friend. He blessed so many hearts and was such a kind, gentle man, always full of joy and laughs. The stories I've heard of his antics were funny, and amazing, and they touched my heart beyond measure. You used him in so many ways and in so many lives, and for that I am one very proud wife."

To think of him now always brings such a huge smile to my face and joy to my heart. My understanding for his departure is still not super clear, but I am seeing that God is in control. And I truly have peace when I lean in and totally trust Him. Who am I to think that I could rule and reign over an entire universe with greater wisdom and direction than Jehovah Himself? God forbid; I can barely guide my two kids! He is a good, good Father and I must learn that freedom of heart comes when I Let Go and Let God. Blessings come in and out of our lives, and though we love some more than others and hate to see them go, we must learn to totally trust our Father God. His love for you is greater than you can ever comprehend. You are His precious child, and He wants to lavish His love on you in so many ways. Wait, and see the goodness of God! Job did, you can too!

Reflection Questions:

Have you recently experienced a loss in your life? If yes, how has your perspective on life and faith changed since the loss of your loved one?

_____

_____

_____

_____

_____

_____

_____

In what ways can you find gratitude for the time you had together?

_____

_____

_____

_____

_____

_____

_____

In what ways can you change your perspective to see the blessings and growth that have come from your journey of grief and healing, despite the pain of losing your loved one?

_____

_____

_____

_____

_____

_____

_____

_____

Worship Encounter:

"Praise You in This Storm"

by Casting Crowns

"Even If" by Mercy Me

"Coming Back" by Hope Darst

The world you see is created by what you focus on. It is never too late to adjust your lens.
~Unknown~

Adjust Your Lens

Kathy Boykin

You know when we take selfies, we usually adjust settings, look at our hair; some we photo shoot; we delete and redo 100 times. You get the picture.

But when you hold the camera looking at your life instead of your appearance, are you adjusting your settings to your past failures?

Are you adjusting your settings to unforgiveness toward someone?

Are you adjusting your settings to the depression from life beating you down?

Are your lenses set on all your yesterdays that never turned out like you planned?

Are your settings stuck on the negative report the Doctor gave you?

Are your settings locked in on the person who walked out of your life?

Look at the settings on your camera. Let's adjust our settings. Let's adjust our settings to see your healing coming that doctors said wouldn't.

Isaiah 53:5 *He was wounded for our transgressions, He was bruised for our iniquities: the chastisement of our peace was upon Him; and with His stripes we are healed.*

Let's adjust our settings to see our betrayer through the eyes of God.

Matthew 22:37-39 *Jesus said unto him, "Thou shalt love the Lord thy God with all thy heart, and with all thy soul, and with all thy mind."*

38 This is the first and great commandment.

39 And the second is like unto it, thou shalt love thy neighbor as thyself.

Let's fix our settings on being happy and living life again.

Psalm 34:18 *"The Lord is nigh unto them that are of a broken heart; and saveth such as be of a contrite spirit."*

Adjust those settings to get back everything you lost.

Joel 2:25 *And I will restore to you the years that the locust hath eaten, the cankerworm, and the caterpillar, and the palmerworm, my great army which I sent among you.*

Adjust those settings to have better days ahead.

Isaiah 40:31 *But they that wait upon the Lord shall renew their strength; they shall mount up with wings as eagles; they shall run, and not be weary; and they shall walk, and not faint.*

Let's adjust that lens when someone walks away to...

I Corinthians 2:9 *"But as it is written, Eye hath not seen, nor ear heard, neither have entered the heart of man, the things which God hath prepared for them that love him."*

So come on and pick that camera back up. Adjust those lenses and start seeing a prettier picture of your tomorrow. Take those old pictures of yesterday and burn them. You now hold a newer camera with a better lens. With better adjusting to be clearer than before. To adjust and focus more on the beauty of your future. Capture your smile walking into your tomorrows knowing God holds you in the palm of His hand.

Isaiah 49:16 *"See, I have engraved you on the palms of my hands; your walls are ever before me."*

Today let's adjust our settings and smile again.

Reflection Questions:

How can I apply the principle of adjusting my focus, as demonstrated in Isaiah 53:5, to view my current challenges through a lens of faith and healing?

_____

_____

_____

_____

_____

_____

Reflecting on Matthew 22:37-39, how might shifting my perspective to see others through God's eyes transform my relationships and interactions with those who have hurt me?

_____

_____

_____

_____

_____

_____

Considering Isaiah 40:31, in what ways can I realign my mindset to anticipate and embrace the better days ahead, trusting in God's promise to renew my strength?

_____

_____

_____

_____

_____

_____

_____

Worship Encounter:

"Promise Keeper" by Hope Darst

"Goodbye Yesterday" by Elevation Rhythm

"New Thing Coming" by Elevation Worship

"If sitting at the feet of Jesus is not the most glorious place for me to be, nothing else will ever fulfill the desires of my heart."
~Back Porch Devotionals by Katie Dietz~

At Your Feet

DeAnna D. Cavenah

One morning while sitting in the presence of the Lord I went in with a heavy burden. I immediately heard in my spirit a song by Clint Brown, "At Your Feet." Which was exactly where I was: At His Feet.

When you give space to the Lord and yield to Him, He opens up your spiritual ears and you can go beyond the noise to hear what the Spirit is saying. The word says that He will sing songs of deliverance over you.

Lyrics to "At Your Feet"

Verse 1
An alabaster box held the costly perfume
She anointed You that day as the fragrance filled the room.
She washed your feet with tears and dried them with her hair.
I know how Mary felt as she was kneeling there.

Refrain
At your feet - At your feet
I humbly bow before You with honor I adore You
At your feet - At your feet
There's no place I'd rather be than at Your feet.

Verse 2
It's hard to understand why life seems unfair.
Lord, I'm carrying this load that I'm not meant to bear.
But You said in Your Word that peace can be found
*If I can find the **courage** just to lay it **ALL** down.*

I want to pull out a few of the bold words from this song to encourage you.

Courage = strength in the face of pain or grief. The quality of mind or spirit that enables a person to face difficulty, danger, pain, etc. without fear.

The opposite of fear is courage, and it is a prerequisite to live a successful life.

Matthew 14:27-28 (AMP) *but immediately He spoke to them, saying, "Take courage it is I! Do not be afraid!" Peter replied to Him, "Lord, if it is (really) you, command me to come to you on the water."*

Don't you hear the Lord beckoning you right now to walk on water? That morning as I sat with the Lord, I heard Him beckoning me to walk on water, but I had been weighed down with cargo that was no longer serving my purpose. He was saying to me, "If you can find the courage, just lay it all down."

In order to find something, you must be willing to be focused and undistracted. His word tells us if we seek, we shall find. And I needed to find courage.

Jeremiah 29:13 (AMP) *Then (with a deep longing) you will seek me and require of me (as a vital necessity) and (you will) find me when you search for me with all your heart.*

ALL = the whole of one's energy or interest. Totality, all that I have. Synonyms = predetermine, complete-entire-full-greatest-outright-perfect-total.

In order to find the courage to lay it **all** down we have to search our **hearts**.

The root of the word **Courage** is Cor- the Latin word for HEART.

We must have a brave heart to allow the Holy Spirit to search out the matters of our heart.

When we have gone through traumatic events in our lives and have gone through the healing process, once we have come through and crossed over to the other side of it, we have to stay alert and wise to the enemy's schemes and tactics. He is very cunning and crafty. He is very patient and will allow time to plot against you and when he sees the opportune time he will hit the trigger button.

One situation, one name, one look, one text, one phone call, one smell, one place, one whatever—it only takes that one circumstance to trigger you and cause you to revert back to the trauma; if we are not armored up we will fall for it. I'd like to say I have passed the test every time but sadly, I have given in to the triggers.

Proverbs 4:23 (TPT) *So above all, guard the affections of your heart for they affect all that you are. Pay attention to the welfare of your innermost being, for from there flows the wellspring of life.*

Heart- the Hebrew word *levav* is the most common word for "heart." It includes our thoughts, our will, our discernment, and our affections.

Wellspring of Life - although most translations have "the issues of life," the Hebrew word *yasa* is actually "seasons," especially springtime. Out of your heart flow the seasons of life. It is our hearts, not our ages or circumstances that shape the seasons of our lives. If our hearts are tender to God, we can live in a perpetual springtime!

Proverbs 4:25-27 (TPT) *Set your gaze on the path before you. With fixed purpose, looking straight ahead, ignore life's distractions. Watch where you're going! Stick to the path of truth, and the road will be safe and smooth before you. Don't* *allow yourself to be sidetracked for even a moment or take the detour that leads to darkness.*

When we are not constantly guarding our hearts, the gates of our mind, will, and emotions, we allow everything to enter in, and we are sure to get distracted and get off the right path, which can easily lead to sin.

I John 3:20-21 (TPT) *Whenever our hearts make us feel guilty and remind us of our failures, we know that God is much greater and more merciful than our conscience and He knows everything there is to know about us. My delightfully loved friends, when our hearts don't condemn us we have a bold freedom to speak face to face with God.*

The face-to-face encounters with God will truly transform us. So however the enemy can keep you from these encounters, he will go out of his way to do it. He tries to make our very own hearts condemn us. It's called self-sabotage.

But friend let me remind you today that you are fully known, fully seen, and fully loved by your Heavenly Father.

There is a higher courtroom for the human heart. It is where grace is enthroned. The very worst that is in us is known by God and He still showers us with mercy, love, and acceptance. This is the greatness of God's grace. He sees beyond the sin of a moment and sees the holy affections of love in those who refuse to turn away from Him. So we should remind ourselves of God's goodness and mercy towards us when we allow ourselves to fall back into sin from the triggers in our hearts, our minds, our will, and our emotions. God is stronger and greater than the accusing voice of our conscience.

Going back to verses 20-23 of Proverbs 4: *Listen carefully, my dear child, to everything I teach you and pay attention to all that I have to say. Fill your thoughts with my words until they penetrate deep into your spirit. Then, as you unwrap my words they will impart true life and radiate health into the very core of your being.*

How many of us are walking around and living spiritually sick, which then leads to physical sickness?

Proverbs 3:1-3 (AMP) *My son, do not forget my teachings, but let your heart keep my commandments; for length of days and years of life (worth living) and tranquility and prosperity (the wholeness of life's blessings) they will add to you. Do not let mercy, kindness, and truth leave you (instead let these qualities define you) bind them (securely) around your *neck, write them on the tablets of your heart.*
* The neck is a symbol of our will and conscience.

So, whatever the enemy is trying to trap you in or trip you up with, whatever he is using as a trigger, go ahead and turn it around on him. Think of it as a trigger on a gun. Turn it on him, pull that trigger, and blow him away. No more to taunt you. See it as an opportunity for victory!

Whatever you have gone through or may be currently going through, it is only a tool for the good. Use it as a weapon to slay!

Romans 8:28 *For we know that all things work together for good to those who love the Lord and who are called according to His purpose.*

Reflection Questions:

What has the Holy Spirit been asking you to lay down with all your heart at his feet? Have you done so? If not, write a prayer of surrender to Him.

_____

_____

_____

_____

_____

In what ways has the enemy been trying to sabotage your focus being on the Lord at all times, listening for His voice? Take time now to turn that against Him and speak the truth of God's Word.

_____

_____

_____

_____

_____

> ### Worship Encounter:
>
> **"At Your Feet"** by Clint Brown
>
> **"Alabaster Heart"** by Bethel and Kalley
>
> **"Altar Call"** by The Belonging

"A Miracle is Possible
Wherever Faith is
Unstoppable!"
~Joshua Mills~

"Faith For a Miracle"

Lacy Saucier

As I sit here writing this, I can't help but get overwhelmed with joy by how blessed I truly am. October 28, 2010, we found out I was pregnant with our third child. In early November, I began to experience heavy abdominal pain. Since that didn't feel normal, I decided to go in to be evaluated. The ER doctor did an ultrasound and found no baby. They didn't act panicked but told me I would need to follow up with my doctor the next day. It was there the journey began.

The doctor did another ultrasound and again, we saw no baby. At that point, I was panicking. The doctor told me either there was a baby in my fallopian tube, or there was no baby at all, which was called a blighted ovum. (Blighted ovum is a fancy way of saying there is an empty gestational sack in the uterus that never grows a baby.) It was heartbreaking because either way, this was bad news. However, I immediately told the doctor I was not willing to do a DNC or any other procedure that would affect my pregnancy negatively. I told him that if I would miscarry, it would have to happen naturally.

While I left devastated and starting to prepare my mind and my heart for whichever of these it would be, and although I heard the doctor, I just couldn't accept it. Something in me just wouldn't receive the report.

Because we had time, we didn't have to make a rushed decision or do anything that would terminate the pregnancy. My doctor was patient and willing to take a couple of extra steps. This led to weekly ultrasounds and blood work every 72 hours to see if there were any changes. Expecting there would soon be a decline in my HGC (hormone gestational count) levels, my doctor sent me for another ultrasound at the hospital to rule out a tubal pregnancy.

I went to the hospital to have the ultrasound and to our surprise, there was no baby in the tube. All that time, my HGC (hormone gestational count) levels were rising perfectly as if it were a normal pregnancy. There was no sign of miscarriage.

After doing blood work and ultrasounds for two weeks, trying hard to have faith and not give up, my doctor said, "Okay, I'm going to send you for the last ultrasound on Thursday to rule out blighted ovum. I am not even sure if your insurance will cover this one, but it will be the last one I can send you for."

Overwhelmed and falling into depression, the trap of the enemy, I waited for Thursday to come. During that time, I didn't answer my phone because most of the people on the other side were coming in agreement with the doctor's report, saying miscarriage was normal and I would get through this. One person even said that my body could be tricked into thinking it was pregnant, and I would have to do the DNC if I wanted to get pregnant in the future. The devil is a liar! I didn't want to hear anything that didn't speak faith into my situation. I had to shut the voices down!

Tuesday night before the last scheduled ultrasound, my three-year-old son was lying on a pallet on the side of my bed, playing with my phone. Because it was bedtime and time to shut the phone off, I took it from him and told him goodnight. As I went to shut down the phone, I realized the Bible app was open and there I saw a scripture that changed the course for me. It was a rhema Word from the Lord.

The thief comes only to steal and kill and destroy. I come that they may have life and have it abundantly. ~John 10:10

At that very moment, an overwhelming sense of peace washed over me. Immediately, I took hold of that scripture and knew deep down inside that everything was okay with my baby. Dread instantly turned into anticipation. I went from dreading Thursday to hardly being able to wait.

The nurse from the doctor's office had called me on Wednesday to let me know exactly what time the ultrasound was scheduled for and to see how I was doing. I told her I was doing fine and that I believed I was going to see my baby on

Thursday. With doubt in her voice, she said, "Oh, I sure hope so."

I replied, "I know so and I'm going to come show you."

Thursday finally came; it was almost time for the ultrasound, and I began to feel sick from worry (of course, the devil was still trying to win). I just started rebuking him and standing on the Word I knew God had given me.

I went into my appointment for the ultrasound, and I realized I was at the wrong hospital. Nobody told me the location changed from where I had been going for all the other appointments. In a panic, I raced across town to the other location, hoping they wouldn't reschedule my appointment. After all the opposition, the "final" ultrasound arrived.

I lay on the table and closed my eyes, just praying and waiting. We did the ultrasound and still, there was no baby. I started to break down, but faith still wanted to rise up. I knew I had a Word from the Lord. Why would He give me a word to stand on if my baby wasn't there?

The technician said, "Let me try one more way." She did another ultrasound, looked at the screen, did a double take, and then turned the computer screen faster than I've ever seen one turn. With a huge smile on her face, she clicked the screen and said "Look, it's your baby!" There was my precious baby girl I had prayed and believed for even when I truly didn't know how. She was so little, only a few weeks into gestation and had just needed more time to show up on an ultrasound.

I had a scheduled doctor's appointment after my ultrasound that day and as my doctor was reading the ultrasound, all he could say was, "This is amazing, and this is the last thing I thought I would see today." He also said, "The nurse who called on Wednesday said that you told her you would see your baby today. I must admit I didn't think that would be the case myself." He even talked about lukewarm faith and said he needed to make some changes for himself.

Our daughter has completed our family in so many ways, and we thank God for her daily.

Here are some takeaways from this:

- ❖ Faith is the catalyst to miracles
- ❖ Walk by faith, not by sight.
- ❖ You can do ALL things through Christ who strengthens you.
- ❖ Just when I was ready to give up, having no strength of my own left, God had a different plan. His plan was LIFE.
- ❖ Speak Life over your circumstances
- ❖ We can Thank God that things don't go according to our plan or even a doctor's plan, but His ways are higher are His plans for us are so much greater.
- ❖ Don't give up right before your miracle!
- ❖ Your bold faith could be the reason someone else chooses to believe and hope again.

Reflection Questions:

Is there an area in your life where your faith is being tested?

_____

_____

_____

_____

_____

What promise has the Lord given you in His Word about this area?

_____

_____

_____

_____

_____

How can you begin to stand on God's promises by faith more boldly?

_____

_____

_____

_____

"**More Than Able**" by Elevation Worship

"**God of Miracles**" by Chris McClarney

"**Another One**" by Elevation Worship

"God is the God of the impossible and the One who can make a miracle out of any situation."
~Joyce Meyer~

God Still Does Miracles:
The Story of God's Beloved Sons John and Wyatt

Candace Havard

John, who is now sixteen, was healed from a rare disease called Hirschsprung's. (Hursh-Sprung). John has had fourteen surgeries total in his life span, all but one under the age of four. The hand of God was all over him during this tough season we found ourselves in. God's hand is still upon John to this day. He almost died and as I write this, I remember it just like it was yesterday.

The doctor came in on New Year's Day and said, "We cannot do anything more for John here. We will need to transfer him to New Orleans Children's Hospital." John was on a ventilator at the time and his little belly looked like a football. Within four hours that same day, we packed up from the hospital room that had been our home for the past three months. They put my baby, not even four months old, on a helicopter since the drive was too long. They weren't even sure he would make it.

They arrived with John at the hospital before I did and immediately started exploratory surgery on him. Hours later I finally got his diagnosis, and that is where, for the next two years we began his journey to healing. The surgeon was sent straight from God. Everything he did during those years was nothing short of a miracle. God's hand was upon John through it all.

At that time, he had two ileostomy bags, peg tubes, and they removed his complete colon, large intestine, and half of his small intestine. John only has thirty centimeters of his small bowel. But looking at him you only see smiles. The Doctor said he wouldn't potty train till around seven years of age, but he potty trained at age two. He had to wear a pull-up of some sort until around age 15. He does not have the sensation we have that tells us to go use the restroom. There were many nights John would have accidents. We would have to strip him, strip all the bedding, give him a bath, etc.

In spite of everything we have gone through with him, God is so good. John plays football and basketball at the time of writing this. He has grown to 6'4". He does not let anything stop him. He is a loving and kind young man who has a powerful testimony. He is a walking, talking, living, breathing miracle.

Wyatt, who is now ten, was healed from a tumor while still in my womb. When my husband and I went to find out what we were having, that is when we found out about the tumor. During this time, there was a gentleman teaching on healing at our church. This gentleman knew things no one did, even to the degree of what side the tumor was on. He prayed over me and my womb. He anointed a cloth and told me to wear it everywhere I went, even to sleep. I did.

One week later, I got the call saying everything was fine— no tumor! The day we found out about the tumor I had to do extensive blood work and they had told me it would take two weeks for the results to come back, but I serve a good God. Not only did I walk in the healing I knew took place on that Wednesday night at church, but I stayed in a peace I can't explain. I knew our son was healed.

When Wyatt was about four months old, my husband noticed something wrong with his eye. We took him in to be checked, They sent us to an eye specialist. The doctor said he had Coloboma—his retinae hadn't fully developed.

Well, fast forward and Wyatt at ten is a pitcher for his baseball team. His eye with 5% vision is the eye that faces the batter and catcher. He throws hard with strikes! Wyatt has blurred vision in this eye, but God is good. John and Wyatt have been touched by God and God is no respecter of persons. If God can do all of that for me and my sons, He will for you. We serve a miracle-working God who still does miracles.

Reflection Questions:

Have you ever witnessed a miracle? If so, describe the experience. If not, are you currently facing something that seems impossible?

_____

_____

_____

_____

_____

How will you remember the works of the Lord moving forward and trust Him for the victory? What is one step you can take to believe for the impossible?

_____

_____

_____

_____

_____

Worship Encounter:

"Wait on The Lord" by Elevation Worship

"Hands of The Healer" by Hope Darst

"WayMaker" by The Pentecostals of Alexandria

When you go through deep waters, I will be with you. When you go through rivers of difficulty, you will not drown. When you walk through the fire of oppression, you will not be burned up; the flames will not consume you.

Isaiah 43:2 NLT

The Crushing in our Normalcy:
"Beau's Story"
Marlena Carlin

It's amazing how you can wake up and start your day, and the normalcy of it all is routine. On any particular day, you can go about your routine with no earthly idea that your normal will soon shake you to your very core.

On one regular Sunday, I awoke, spent time with the Lord, got the kids dressed, went to church, and then to eat after. That particular Sunday we had a family swimming birthday party to attend in the afternoon. Nothing felt off; the kids were excited.

At the party, everybody was having a blast. The kids were swimming, splishing and splashing, jumping in and out of the water. Total fun! Then it was time to cut the cake inside. My husband took off our son's life jacket and they went in the house. I was already inside. My husband and I went back outside to the pool area to get a towel for our son. My husband heard the voice of the Lord, "Look in the water."

"There's a child in there," my husband told me before he dove into the pool. He went down eight feet where I later learned Beau had been flat on his back with his arms spread out at the bottom of the pool. When my husband resurfaced, I recognized the child's clothes. It was my child.

I wouldn't have wanted it to be anybody's child, but suddenly, this was *my* reality, Beau was lifeless, his lips and body bluish, , his eyes glazed over and fixed to the sky with no blinking. My reality was—he was dead—he drowned! I was screaming, "NO, GOD, NO!" and pulling my hair out.

Our family came outside and my husband and another gentleman started trying to revive him. My niece was holding me, speaking faith into me, and praying. Others were screaming in tongues, praying, and children were in the house praying, I felt like glass about to shatter, I heard them saying, "It's not working," over and over, and my husband was screaming for me to get away from the scene. My niece and I looked away for a moment, but I wasn't leaving that scene.

We were down to the wire at that point, and my mind was reeling with the reality that my four-year-old baby was gone. Just before, I thought he was in the house getting cake. I can't honestly say my faith was where it needed to be, I couldn't think straight, I couldn't even pray. I was in such shock as though lightning had just struck me, I could only shake and scream. but everybody around me spoke faith and prayed, and in that moment, nothing in this world mattered but saving Beau.

Someone called our churches and family not there, and they were in one accord with us: that this child would live and breathe again. The next thing I knew, there was a doctor on the scene; he happened to be on his way to church and was running behind. The doctor came and administered CPR, and it took a little time, which seemed like eternity to me with my heart shredding to pieces.

That was my baby lying there. How was I supposed to live without my baby? The crushing, the shattering. It was real.

When I was giving birth to Beau completely naturally, I was screaming, "I can't do this!" and the nurses said, "You have no choice."

Well here I was again screaming, shaking, shattering with no choice (and the Lord used someone in the medical field this time too). "God's willing vessel." After the doctor noticed Beau's tongue was interfering (he had bit down on his tongue, and his jaw had already locked) my husband pried his jaw open to release his tongue back into place. The doctor resumed administering CPR. And just like when I was giving birth to my baby, he came back into this world, though a little differently, this time with the breath of God.

After a few moments, my little boy started spitting up, moving, and blinking. God had resurrected my baby—he was reborn—and just like that moment after his natural birth of, *'Phew I did it!'* there was a, *'Phew!'* released on that property. But it wasn't me who did it; it was without a doubt our God! Finally, after all the crushing, after 10-12 minutes of my little boy being dead, I could breathe again, everybody could breathe again, Beau was breathing again.

If you ever find yourself, in a down-to-the-wire situation, a moment or period of being shattered., crushed, feeling like you can't breathe, let Beau's rebirth be a vessel of hope: that no matter what the crushing looks like, even if it's death, hold steady; that God can and will get you through this and you will get the "Phew, we can breathe again," moment, and you will know without a doubt that it was God.

As for me and my house, HE gets all the honor and glory. One way we honor the Lord is by giving away dinosaurs. My son absolutely adores dinosaurs, and we are so grateful he's alive. My family gives them out as a reminder of hope. The fact we get to have the privilege of giving them to people instead of putting them on a grave—how can we not share "Beau's story"?

I pray that each person this story reaches will be given a hope that God is still on the throne. If He can resurrect my child from the dead, then He can get you through whatever it is that you or a loved one are facing! Miracles are still happening!

Reflection Questions:

Reflect on a time in your own life when you felt as though you were being crushed. How did you respond? What was the outcome?

_____

_____

_____

_____

_____

Considering Beau's story, how can you apply this testimony to your life? Consider writing a prayer of surrender and faith to the Lord.

_____

_____

_____

_____

_____

Worship Encounter:
"Miracle Child" by Brandon Lake
"Million Little Miracles" by Elevation Worship
"All Of a Sudden" by Elevation Worship

You are Enough.
You have always
been Enough.
You will always be
Enough.
~Etta Arlene~

Coffee with My 15-Year-Old Self

Stefanee Tolbert

"The Lord is close to the brokenhearted and saves those who are crushed in spirit." — Psalm 34:18

I sat across from her—the girl in the lime green GAP hoodie, the one that probably hadn't seen a washing machine in weeks. She fidgeted with her sleeves, unsure of herself, convinced she wasn't enough. She didn't know yet that she was smart. She didn't know yet that she was strong. And she definitely didn't know the love of Christ.

She was broken, exhausted from carrying burdens too heavy for teenage shoulders. Depression had taken up residence in her mind, and the prescription bottle in her bag wasn't doing much to evict it. She thought life was just something to survive. But I leaned in, smiling, because I knew something she didn't—her life had always been something worth living.

I told her that next year, at 16, she would meet her future husband. She wouldn't know it then, but one day, years later, he would be leading worship from the stage, and she would be at the altar, singing the prayer of salvation as she led a deaf boy to Christ. In that moment, he would look down and just know—she was the one.

I told her life wouldn't always be easy—at all. There would be heartbreak, loss, and moments that felt impossible. There would be nights where she would cry herself to sleep and days where she would feel like she was never going to get it right. She would face rejection, failure, and seasons where she would wonder if God even saw her.

But then I told her something else—something she could barely believe. "The good," I said, "will far outweigh the bad."

One day, she and her husband would raise four incredible children and serve the Lord as a family. Together, they would build a life they loved. She would experience deep joy, true love, and a purpose greater than she could ever imagine.

And then I told her something that made her laugh in disbelief. "One day," I said, "you're going to start a school."

She shook her head. "Me? The girl who failed Algebra I last year? The one who has spent more Saturdays in detention than she can count?"

"Yes, you," I said. "It will start small, but it will grow into something that changes thousands of lives. Turns out, you were never a failure. You were just a leader in the making."

She didn't believe me at first. And honestly, I didn't expect her to. When you're in the middle of the struggle, it's hard to believe that God is actually working all things together for your good. But He is.

Because that's who He is.

The God who saw her in the brokenness is the same God who carried her into healing. The God who watched her crumble is the same God who built her back up. The God who felt distant is the same God who was closer than she ever realized.

And He is that same God for you today.

Maybe you feel like that girl in the lime green Gap hoodie. Maybe you feel like you don't belong, like you're too broken, like you're just trying to survive. Maybe you've convinced yourself that your mistakes have disqualified you, that your failures define you, that your past is too messy for God to do anything meaningful with your life.

But let me tell you what I told her:

Keep going.

There is beauty on the other side of this pain. You are not too broken, and you are not forgotten. God is still writing your story. And trust me—you're going to love it there.

Reflection Questions:

Think back to a time when you felt like you weren't enough. How has God proven to you that your life has always been worth living?

_____

_____

_____

_____

_____

Have you ever believed a lie about yourself that God later disproved? What was it, and how has He rewritten that narrative?

_____

_____

_____

_____

_____

If you could sit across from your younger self today, what encouragement would you give?

_____

_____

_____

_____

What dreams has God placed inside of you that seem too big or impossible? How can you take a small step toward them today?

_____

_____

_____

_____

_____

How has God used your past failures or struggles to shape the person you are today?

_____

_____

_____

_____

_____

Heavenly Father, thank You for never letting me go, even when I couldn't see Your hand in my life. Thank You for reminding me that I was never a mistake, never too broken, and never too far gone. Help me to embrace the truth that You have a purpose for me and that my story is still being written. Give me the faith to trust You even when I don't understand. And when I look back, let me see how You were there all along. I trust You, Lord. Lead me into the life You've created me to live. Amen.

Worship Encounter:

"Rescue" by Lauren Daigle

As you listen, let the words remind you that God has always been near, fighting for you, rescuing you, and calling you forward. No matter where you've been, His love has never let you go.

YOU ARE beautiful
YOU ARE brave
YOU ARE loved
YOU ARE important
YOU ARE capable
YOU ARE ENOUGH

You Are Enough

Catherine Deere

Going through childhood abuse changed my life in so many ways. I stayed to myself and did not trust anyone. I was taught to keep my mouth shut and hide all evidence of the abuse. Through the trauma, I became very angry and someone totally different from the person I intended to be. Life was dictated for me by someone else's cruelty. I felt like I didn't know who I was or what I was to do with my life. I actually tried to end my life because I didn't have a way out of all the abuse.

When you are abused, you feel like there is no hope for your life to ever become anything good. I felt rejected, lonely, unwanted, abandoned, unlovable, used, ugly, bad, and more. This stopped my dreams and my chance to know what love truly was. It blocked my joy and peace, my comfort and understanding the love God had for me. I eventually turned my back on God. BUT GOD! God changed all of this for me.

Even though I have experienced such trauma that no one will ever know the depth of, I have found joy and peace in God. God was there with me through it all; I just didn't realize it until I received my healing. I now understand the love God has for me. I will never give up on my dreams and you shouldn't either because we serve a loving God.

God reminds me, and I am reminding you, that:

"You are enough!"

"You are loved!" and

"You are beautiful!"

When I'm going through a battle, I go to God to guide me, and He helps me stay strong to stand firm in my faith. I have found some trustworthy friends to stand with me, help me up, and pray for/with me. But knowing that God will never leave me has changed my life. I encourage you to never give up, continue moving forward, and expect things to change in your situation. I would have never dreamed I would be so deep in love with Jesus after I turned my back on Him as a child stuck in my prison. I found hope in God, and I am no longer a slave of the mindset the abuser taught me, I am free!

Ponder this: If God did it for me, He will do it for you (Romans 2:11).

Reflection Questions:

How does understanding that you are enough change your perspective on past traumas and current challenges?

_____

_____

_____

_____

_____

In what ways can you remind yourself daily of your worth and the love that God has for you?

_____

_____

_____

_____

_____

How can you integrate the affirmation, "You are enough," into your interactions with others to promote healing and confidence?

_____

_____

_____

_____

Deeper Truth:

Galatians 4:7: You are free, no longer a slave.

2 Corinthians 6:18: God is your Father.

1 Peter 5:9: Stand firm.

Isaiah 40:31: Trust in the Lord, your strength will be renewed.

Philippians 4:13: God gives you strength.

Worship Encounter:

"No Longer Slaves" by Jonathan and Melissa Helser

"Thank God I do" by Lauren Daigle

"Trust In God" by Elevation Worship

"You're Still God" by Philippa Hanna

"People pleasing hides
the real you"
~Unknown~

"No one can make you
feel inferior without
your consent."
~Eleanor Roosevelt~

People Pleaser

DeAnna D. Cavenah

And then one day a light shone brightly and beamed down on this verse...

"I'm obviously not trying to flatter you or water down my message to be popular with men, but my supreme passion is to please God. For if all I attend to do is people please, I would fail to be a true servant of Christ." ~ Galatians 1:10 (TPT)

I'm amazed that no matter how many times I read through the scriptures, there is always going to be that particular verse that just jumps off the page, at just the right time.

I want to ask you these questions right here in the beginning...

Are you a people pleaser?

Do you thrive on the approval of others?

Do you feel you must perform in a certain way that gets people's attention in order for them to accept or like you?

Ponder these for just a few moments before moving forward.

If you answered YES to any of these three questions, you can be free from that bondage today.

I'm not proud to say this, but I have been guilty of saying YES to all three of those questions myself.

When we allow ourselves to be a people pleaser or seek approval we become their bond slave. We are in a self-made prison and have given control of our lives to another person. My friend, we should never give that much control to anyone. In all honesty, we have just made that person an idol.

God says He will have no other idols before Him. It's even listed as one of the Ten Commandments. He is a jealous God, and He is passionate about what is His. You have been bought with the precious blood of Jesus, and He says you are His.

This is the Amplified version of Galatians 1:10: *"Am I now trying to win favor and approval of men, or of God? If I were still trying to be popular with men, I would not be a bond-servant of Christ."*

Let's above all else seek to please God in all we say and do. If we don't, we allow seeds of rejection to take root in our lives.

Because, after all, let's be honest and not kid ourselves, not everyone is going to like us, approve of us, or like what we say or do. You are only setting yourself up for failures and rejections—some that may take years to recover from.

You and I don't have to perform for anyone. Don't exhaust yourself. Time is the only thing you can never get back, so don't waste another minute on things or people that don't matter. Not everyone is a part of your assignment or journey. Let the Lord capture your gaze. Don't get stuck on what your natural eyes can see, for these things are only temporary; the things which are unseen are eternal.

Your job is not to keep everyone happy. When you think about it, Jesus was nailed to the cross because he refused to do what people expected and demanded from Him. He demonstrated the ultimate example of pleasing the Father and not people.

You have been called by God to fulfill His purposes during your lifetime. You simply will not be fruitful or flourish if you spend your life trying to please people. The only opinion that matters Is the Lord's.

Deeper Truth:
Deuteronomy 5:7-10 (AMP)
Isaiah 43:1 (AMP)
2 Corinthians 4:18 (TPT)

Reflection Questions:

In what areas of my life have I been seeking the approval of others more than God's approval?

_____

_____

_____

How can I shift my focus from trying to make everyone happy to fulfilling God's purpose for my life?

_____

_____

_____

What steps can I take to trust in God's plan and opinion over the opinions of people around me?

_____

_____

_____

Worship Encounter:

"**Accepted**" by Calvary Worship

"**The Truth**" by Megan Woods

"**Made for More**" by Josh Baldwin

Thrive
verb
1: to grow vigorously; FLOURISH
2: to gain in wealth or possessions; PROSPER
3: to progress toward or realize a goal despite or because of circumstances
"My mission in life is not merely to survive, but to THRIVE."
~Maya Angelou~

Thriving in the "Not Where I Thought I'd Be"
Bethany Taylor

"Be strong, and of good courage. Do not be afraid, nor dismayed, for the Lord your God is with you wherever you shall go" ~ Joshua 1:9 (my memorized version.)

We've all heard the saying, "I may not be where I thought I'd be, but I'm exactly where I prayed to be,", and most of us have felt the bittersweet sting of understanding exactly what that means in some area of our lives. Maybe the sting is from a marriage that didn't work out, or a neglectful family relation where hard boundaries had to be made. For some it's a career path that got put on hold, putting in hard work to create a life you didn't have an example of, or learning to embrace life on your own after years of a full house.

As for me, I have ended up "not where I thought I would be" in all those examples of failed expectations. The words of Joshua 1:9 have gotten me through many different challenges and changes in life. But it took me many years of just going through the motions, trying to survive a life I never thought I would have, to fully understand that, like happiness, thriving is a choice. It's the daily choice to let God Walk WITH me that builds my strength so that I will not be dismayed when life doesn't work out my way, and that gives me the courage to not fear when I am walking a different path than the one I planned.

Many of us end up just living our lives stuck in the "not where I thought I'd be" mentality, even if we look like we are thriving from a worldly standard. God's true thriving, though, means the growing, prospering, and flourishing, not of things, but of our soul. That may look like not being afraid to walk into new groups courageously to find one that brings out your best. Sometimes it's being strong enough to retreat in solitude with God instead of being upset to miss a social occasion. Speaking affirmations over yourself, unhinged pursuits of what makes you feel close to Holy Spirit, not being afraid to give up our worldly expectations in pursuit of His divine destiny, all help our soul thrive.

Reflection Questions:

What area of my life do I feel I'm not where I wanted to be, but am where I once prayed to be?

_____

_____

_____

What are some practices I can put into place to change my perspective from just surviving to thriving?

_____

_____

_____

Worship Encounter:

"Everything Belongs"

by Cory Asbury

"Always On Time" by Elevation Worship

"God is in This Story" by Katy Nichole and Big Daddy Weave

God might not
answer our prayers
the way we expect
Him to, but He
always answers our
prayers the way He
ought to.
~Hunter Beless~

"Not Knowing" Space

Angela Broussard

As I was driving in my first "mom" SUV with two toddlers, ages three and five, in the back seat with emotional, behavioral, and physical challenges, needless to say, I was feeling extremely overwhelmed. I was a 52-year-old woman with little experience in how to care for children. As they screamed and slapped each other, I felt I was in a fog and asked myself, "How did I get here?"

CPS asked my husband and I if we wanted to adopt these children since they would probably be available for adoption soon. It was my dream come true: having children and a family after 30+ years of being barren, and there I was, being proposed with this question.

'But this is not what I prayed for, I prayed for children but not this.' Yet this was my dream. . I cried so many nights for this. I had sadness and pain I couldn't explain to anyone. I began to question and try to reason it out. *'You're 52 years old and*

you want children?' How could I not want what was right in front of me, practically delivered to my door?

We had waited three years to be certified to adopt only to have a hurricane destroy the paperwork. *'Lord, what is going on? Maybe you're slamming the door shut. Maybe we're too old and I'll always have this pain and shame.'* Then three weeks later, we got a call from someone asking if we would foster these two toddlers. Now, with the kids, would I crash and burn under the pressure of my dream?

None of this makes sense
52-year-old mother
Can't control the children
Chaos
Husband working out of town and can't help me
I was scared to death to say yes!
I was scared to death to say no!

All I could do was keep moving forward because I had no answer. I was feeling alone; other moms with toddlers were so young with mommy friends. *'Where do I fit in here*?' Most days I was in a daze. I just got up and kept moving forward.

The Lord reminded me of what Joyce Meyer once said, "As you keep moving forward with no answer, the answer will unfold before you." That was such a revelation to me in that moment because I had no answers. I knew God was with me, but the chaos was almost unbearable.

"Lord, where is my promised land?" All these seasons, all this grieving. This song would come on the radio, and I felt God so strongly in the car even with the kids screaming in the back seat as tears would roll down my cheeks. It was one of the hardest things I've done in my entire life but at the same time, the most rewarding. The children ended up with their father and grandmother, and I am still a huge part of their lives. I am now a mom and grandmother. It healed my shame and broken heart, and I am forever grateful. God knew I wouldn't want to start a family at 52 years of age.

Just because it's not making sense and it seems like chaos, doesn't mean it's not part of your journey to your promised land. Don't forfeit your promised land; the best is yet to come. The best things in life are on the other side of your fear. God knows what you need more than you do. He knows what will bring you the most fulfillment more than you do.

As I look back now, I can proudly say I never quit or gave up. I have such joy and fulfillment in my life. You can't always go by what you see in front of you because God is doing something much bigger in you that you cannot see.

Deeper Truth:
Psalm 84:11
Psalms 37:23-24

Reflection Questions:

Feeling like you will never get to your promised land is completely normal. Where are you in this process and what does it look like?

_____

_____

_____

Explain a time in your life when you prayed and waited for something but when God answered it didn't look anything like you prayed for.

_____

_____

_____

What scripture comes to mind when you think of God's faithfulness in your life?

_____

_____

_____

Lord God, you have never left me nor will you. Help me to expect the goodness of who you are to fall on my life. Amen.

<u>Worship Encounter:</u>

"Promised Land" by TobyMac

"Symphony" by Switch

"Gonna Be Alright" by Ryan Ellis

"There Was Jesus" by

Zach Williams and Dolly Parton

No life is more
secure than a life
surrendered to God.
~Unknown~

Surrender

Natalie Fitkin

"And continue to walk surrendered to the extravagant love of Christ." ~ Ephesians 5:2

God's Word is clear that the life of a disciple of Jesus is a life of surrender. Surrender implies submission, yielding, and relinquishing control.

Relinquish control? But, "I've got this!" Being my own lord is how I describe it. I call the shots, do things my way, try to control people and circumstances. The problem is that this gives a false sense of hope and it's exhausting! It has cost me more than I want to admit, including sleep, health, joy, and peace.

"Will you lay down your crown?" is the question that I hear within me. My flesh was offended by the question, yet I knew I was being confronted with truth. Confrontation. Life has a way of confronting you, doesn't it? It quickly reveals that you are not in control.

One August morning, I found myself there.

Living close to the Gulf of Mexico, it is not unusual to evacuate because of an impending hurricane. My family of four packed a few clothes, held hands in our living room, and prayed before we left. Two days later, I received the call and the pictures. Our home was shattered to pieces. In that moment, I had the opportunity to put what I could control to work: my response to the circumstance and the attitude of my heart.

This experience revealed a lot to me about myself. People and circumstances have a way of doing that. They reveal both strengths and weaknesses you never realized you had.

There was a new level of surrender confronting me, a new level of trust in God's love and faithfulness that I would learn to walk in. Surrendering to the love of Christ, I must warn you, gets ugly, messy, and is quite undignified. I learned that it was okay to not be okay as long as I didn't stay there. Lies I had believed were revealed and walls of self-protection I had built in my heart began to crumble. The love of God revealed to me that my broken house uncovered my broken heart, the very thing God wanted to heal.

A new house was built. God provided and He gets the glory. And as I cooperated with Holy Spirit, things that were keeping me from walking in the freedom Jesus purchased for me were processed out of my life. That's what surrendering to the love of Christ will do- free you from yourself.

Surrendering to God's love includes trusting Him to work in ways you cannot see and revealing God's love to others.

Reflection Questions:

What area of your life have you been trying to control that needs to be surrendered to God?

_____

_____

_____

What Scripture in God's Word will help you relinquish control in this process of surrender?

_____

_____

_____

How can you reveal God's love to others as you learn to trust Him in this area of your life?

_____

_____

_____

Worship Encounter:

"Crowns Down" by Gateway Worship
and Josh Baldwin

"At Your Feet" by
Casting Crowns

It only takes God
one moment to
change everything in
your life.
~DeVon Franklin~

In a Moment

Shanyetta Hypolite

Ever wanted something so badly, and the more you prayed, the more things seemed to get worse?

During a particular season of my life, I had a four-year-old son who wanted a sibling desperately, and I wanted so badly to give him one, but there was trouble in my marriage and in my body. Part of my trouble was that I was having difficulty conceiving another child. I thought, *'Maybe I'm thinking about it too much or there's too much stress at work.'* Yeah, that's it right? Wrong! My doctor had declared me to be infertile. How was that even possible? I had a condition called PCOS: polycystic ovary syndrome, and I was severely anemic. For two months, I had a menstrual cycle! And then it happened a second time for another two months!

So needless to say, I could not be intimate with my husband, and he was clearly irritated by that. How could I be like the woman with the issue of blood in the Bible? I mean I went to church. I read my Bible. I didn't drink or smoke and I was faced with this huge mountain. I was depressed, stressed, and a mess!

Then one Sunday, my pastor was preaching on the four things not satisfied in Proverbs 30:15-16. When I heard him say them, I felt convicted for not being grateful for my son, Kristopher. Soon after, there was a healing evangelist who came to our church. During the service, he called out many illnesses and was calling people to go forward, but I felt I could not go because I would be really embarrassed. Yet he stretched his hands forward and my faith latched on! Immediately I felt the blood flow slow down. '*Is this really happening*?' Indeed, it was!

After that, I begin to repent, pray, and spend more intimate time with the Lord. He comforted me and led me to a new OB/GYN, who performed a procedure. Soon after that, I begin to have a normal monthly cycle. January came and, in a moment when my husband and I decided to go separate ways, I found out I was pregnant! In that moment, the Lord began to repair my marriage and He gave our family the desires of our hearts.

God's timing is absolutely perfect! His faithfulness endures forever!

Reflection Questions:

Can you recall a moment in your life when you experienced a significant change or transformation?

_____

_____

How did you see God's hand in that moment?

_____

_____

_____

How can you open yourself up to trust in God's timing, even when it seems like things are not going according to your plans?

_____

_____

_____

What steps can you take to cultivate a deeper faith and belief that God can change your circumstances in an instant?

_____

_____

_____

_____

_____

Deeper Truth:
Psalm 37:4

Worship Encounter:
"God Has a Way"
by Martha Munizzi
"God, Turn It Around"
by Jon Reddick
"Promises" by Maverick City

"God will not permit any troubles to come upon us unless He has a specific plan by which a great blessing can come out of the difficulty."
~ Peter Marshall~

Trials and Tribulations

DeAnna D. Cavenah

A lot can happen in a day, in an hour, in just one moment. You can have a wonderful day turn bad in just an instant. You can have a long-time friendship dissolve with just one word. Sometimes life is this way. It's like trying to hold water in your hand; somehow, it's going to leak through leaving your hand empty with only the dampness that water once existed there.

We walk around in life with a lot of "what used to be" attitudes or "remember when" thoughts having no ability or power to change or control those situations! Sometimes the hardest situations in life are the ones that were not your fault at all, but were brought on by another person's actions; yet you are the one that must suffer the consequences of it. It's an even harder thing to remain silent and allow others to believe something that is absolutely not truth about you or someone you love.

So, the question is: What do you do in these situations? How do you move forward or overcome? From experience, time and time again, I wish I could say it's easy and give you steps 1, 2, and 3 to recover from such disappointment. The hard truth is that it's never easy if you've experienced it one time or twenty times. Trials and tribulations; no one wants them but none of us are exempt from them. By definition, this means: troubles and events that cause tests of one's patience or endurance: difficult experiences, problems, etc.

Synonyms include: adversity, grief, heartache, misery, misfortune, woe, ordeal, burden, care, trouble, and oppression.

I don't know about you, but I don't like the sound of any of those words. But there is an answer for every one of them, and it can be found in God's Word. Seek the Lord in all matters, seek to please Him and Him alone. Stay true to what you know is true, just, and pure.

Don't seek revenge or vindication. God alone is the Righteous Judge and when it looks like the other person is doing well, just know that they too are going to face some sort of hardship. Don't become so fixated on the problem or situation that you are stuck there. Don't look at the things that are seen in the natural for they are only temporary. Do what you know to do, and not what you feel. You matter to God. God is moved by the feelings of your heart, and He is acquainted with your sorrow. You are not alone in this.

Reflection Questions:

Can you recall a moment in your life when you faced a significant trial or tribulation?

_____

_____

_____

How did you manage to endure through it, and what lessons did you learn?

_____

_____

_____

How do you typically respond to moments of adversity?

_____

_____

_____

Are there ways you can improve your approach to better navigate future challenges?

_____

_____

_____

How does knowing that God is acquainted with your sorrow provide comfort during difficult times?

_____

_____

Can you recall a specific moment when you felt His presence in your suffering?

_____

_____

_____

How do you feel knowing that seeking God's guidance and comfort in His Word when faced with hardships will strengthen your faith and resilience?

_____

_____

Deeper Truth:
Romans 5:3-5 (TPT)
Romans 12:19 (TPT)

<u>**Worship Encounter:**</u>
"When Trials Come"
by Keith and Kristyn Getty
"Through It All" by Selah
"My Defender" by Jeremy Camp

There is
Always,
Always,
Always,
A
but God.
~Lisa Appelo~

But God...

Connie Book

Thirty-eight years ago, we were expecting our first child. We were Just a couple of college kids wanting to get our family started and so very excited about our bundle of joy on the way. It was a rainy Friday in July when we welcomed our baby girl. She was 8 lbs 7 oz with a head full of hair. Brittney Lynn was beautiful. She started nursing right away. The doctor said she was a very healthy baby.

Saturday, when the doctor did his routine check, he said there was something he didn't like. He didn't know what, but something was amiss. "I'm going to put her in the NICU so we can start an IV just in case we need it."

I was devastated. The thought of my baby in intensive care was so scary. I was discharged from the hospital on Sunday. We stayed with Brittney for a while, then went home, and I took a quick nap before we went back to the hospital. The time away seemed forever. She seemed so vulnerable in the bassinet with an IV in her little arm.

We went back home for the night. About three a.m., we got a call from the hospital: get up there fast, Brittney was not doing well. I panicked. It seemed to take forever to get to the hospital. When we arrived, a doctor was doing a blood transfusion on her. He told us it didn't look good. I spent my time talking to her, letting her know I was there, kissing her tiny face.

I remember being in a small room right outside the NICU praying and singing "Jesus loves the little children" and begging Him not to let our baby die. Around 10 a.m. , we had a consultation with the doctor. He told us her chances of making it were less than 5%. I couldn't believe it! It just couldn't be! I went back to be with her, and she opened her eyes and looked at me. I told her I was there for her, that I loved her so very much. Our precious baby died about an hour later. We were devastated!

We had to go to the funeral home and pick out a casket. '*Is this really happening? God why did you let our baby die...why?*' Any parent who has had to look at their own child lying in a casket knows the unique heartache. After the funeral our parents came over and we disassembled her crib and packed up her clothes, toys and all the baby items. Within no time at all it was all gone. But the pain in my heart had only just begun.

I had been away from God for some time and after her death, I was mad at him. Every time I saw another mother with her baby I would cry out in my heart, '*Why did she get to keep her baby?! Why did you take my baby?!*'

I just didn't understand. Have you ever been MAD at God? It sounds like such a strange statement, doesn't it? But if I am to be honest, I was mad. In my grief I just couldn't understand why He would let that happen! But God! He saw me in my grief and was there for me. My anger soon turned to longing. Longing to make sure I made heaven my home. Not only to be with our precious baby girl but to be forever with our Heavenly Father forever. He met me in my grief, my anger, and loved me with an everlasting love. "I'm here for you; you do not have to go through this alone"

One year later I gave birth to another baby girl—a precious gift from our Lord! She didn't replace Brittney, no child can replace another, but she was a beautiful God-sent gift.

I'm here to tell you, when you are in a devastating time, turn to our precious Lord. He will see you through your heartache. He loves you; He cries with you. He lifts you up and keeps you afloat. Like Peter, you may think you will drown but take His hand! It's always extended out for you!

"And God shall wipe away all tears from their eyes and there shall be no more death, nor sorrow nor shall there be any more pain, for the former things are passed away" ~ Revelations 21:4

Reflection Questions:

Have you been mad at God? Is there an area you haven't surrendered or maybe even haven't forgiven God for allowing in your life? Take a moment to journal all of it to the Lord.

_____

_____

_____

_____

_____

Have you encountered others who have gone through a similar trial as yours with a different response or outcome?

_____

_____

_____

_____

_____

In what ways have you grown and learned more about God through the trials in your life?

_____

_____

_____

How can you cast your cares on the Lord more fully moving forward and respond in faith during future trials?

_____

_____

_____

_____

_____

Worship Encounter:

"Why God" by Austin French

"Thy Will" by Hillary Scott

"I am not alone" by Kari Jobe

What you feed your
soul is what you
harvest with your
actions.
~Shannon L. Alder~

Feed Your Soul

Toni Petrofes

Are you drowning in the sea of humanity, lost in a world without love, listening to the voices of disapproval and negativity, and not understanding your need for love, affection, significance, attention, and acceptance?

Then feed your soul.

What does that look like?

"Beloved, I pray that in all respects you may prosper and be in good health, just as your soul prospers." ~ 3 John 2.

God created us as tridimensional beings: body (physical), spirit (love), and soul (emotional). God's word is a sword that will heal your soul; it divides your soul and removes that which needs to be removed and replaces it with His love. (Hebrews 4:12)

Are you pursuing a mirage in your attempt at life, passionately seeking illusions from a loveless society? If so, your soul is dehydrated, and you're walking through a desert. Only your Creator can feed your soul.

So, speak to your soul! David did.

Why are you in despair, oh my soul?
And why have you become disturbed within me?
Hope in God, for I shall again praise Him
For the help of his presence. ~ Psalm 42:5

Again and again, David fed his soul.

O God, you are my God; I shall seek you earnestly.
My soul thirsts for You, my flesh yearns for you,
In a dry and weary land where there is no water. ~ Psalm 63:1

Why? If you are whole on the inside, you do not have to pretend on the outside.

The Lord restores my soul. ~ Psalm 23:3

For: *"You shall love the Lord your God with all your heart (spirit) and with all your soul (emotion) and with all your might (bodily strength)."* ~ Deuteronomy 6:5.

It is always your choice. You can be inactive and remain ignorant of your soul's needs, which results in your soul existing in brokenness, emptiness, and loneliness. You can be reactive to your soul's needs and fill your life with dysfunction: sexual promiscuity, pornography, fantasy, self-ambition, drugs, overindulgence in areas of money, food, alcohol, work, play, etc. always trying to feed that soul with junk food that never satisfies, but only asks for more.

You can be proactive with your soul; learn to love God, love yourself, and love all those God puts in your path. Look for ways to proactively fill your world with love that overflows out of you and into the hearts of others.

Think of this phrase: "I love you." It is the most abused phrase on the planet. It is spoken with such frivolity. "Love" is a verb; It does things. It gives, protects, cherishes, forgets offenses; it looks for ways to be kind, generous, respectful, considerate, and welcoming. It speaks words of kindness and encouragement. Is this your soul?

Take your favorite dog. Do you think he/she loves you? Most would say an absolute, "Yes!" But he has never said, "I love you." He is always there, anxiously waiting for you to come home, watching you leave, wagging his tail, following you everywhere, laying at your feet, trying to lick your face, trying to spend every minute of the day with you, warning you of strangers, and protecting you from enemies. And yet, he never says a word. So, if you want your soul to be healthy, feed your soul with God's Word, and learn to love proactively and unconditionally.

Reflection Questions:

In what ways can I actively seek to nourish my soul with God's word, and how might this practice change my daily life?

_____

_____

_____

Reflect on the meaning of loving God, yourself, and others proactively. How can you demonstrate this love in your interactions and relationships?

_____

_____

_____

Can you identify the "junk food" you might be feeding your soul? What steps can you take to replace these with healthier, more fulfilling spiritual disciplines?

_____

_____

_____

Worship Encounter:

"It is Well with My Soul" hymn by Horatio Spafford and Phillip Bliss

"Whatever It Costs" by Rachel Morley

And I heard God ask, "Who will I send?"
And I said, "Here I am! Send me!"
~Isaiah 6:8~

Who Will Go?

Rena Beadle

In the fall of 2021, I embarked on a very unexpected journey. During a Zoom staff meeting, we were told that if George, a male, wanted to identify as a female and be called "Suzy," then we must call him "Suzy." However, we were NOT to inform his parents of this situation. And, if we talked to his parents, we must address George by his legal name.

After hearing this directive, I froze—deaf to the rest of what felt like endless chatter. However, later in the hallway, I could hear teachers faintly expressing their personal views. Some were horrified, and others were apathetically succumbing to the request because it was just what many did.

My husband and I have five sons. Four of our sons are married, and we welcome new grandchildren annually.

Throughout 2020, our family observed school boards across the nation ignoring parental concerns about transgender surgeries and hormone treatments on minors. And then the matter was at home, in Texas.

According to our State Representative, there were six-month waiting lists of children signing up for breast removals, and these were happening practically in our backyards. I couldn't sleep, so I prayed.

A few days later, I approached one of our counselors, sadly confiding about how burdened I was about the charge we'd been given for our students.

She replied, "Mrs. Beadle, we are just as flabbergasted as you! We even called the school district to make sure this was what they wanted us to say. And they told us to say it word-for-word!"

'Jesus, help me,' I silently prayed. I sadly looked into her eyes and said, "You understand this is moving towards body mutilation. There is a scripture that says, 'If anyone causes one of these little ones—those who believe in me—to stumble, it would be better for them to have a large millstone hung around their neck and to be drowned in the depths of the sea.'" [Matthew 18:6 NIV]

I continued by telling her, "I will not refer to George as 'Suzy,' and I will tell his parents. The administration can walk me out of here, but I will not do this," I then silently walked away.

Soon afterward, I felt compelled to reach out to our State Representative, Steve Toth, to share my story. His eyes widened in shock and disbelief! I didn't realize until later that State Representatives collaborate extensively with their county's school superintendents. Representative Toth was unaware that this was going on in our Montgomery County schools. He asked if I would give him the date and time of the Zoom staff meeting so his legal department could find the particular slide in question.

After sending him the information, the journey began. Excuses piled up endlessly, like: "Rep. Toth, the Gender Dysphoria student will kill themself if we refuse to allow them to transition." Interestingly, however, the research said differently.

I was later invited to share my testimony at our church following a documentary that had just been released from California. The audience was shocked as parents in the documentary detailed the negative impact of California's approach to transgender minors, including tragic suicides. My teacher friends, who I had invited to attend, later told of one of their students who had expressed a desire to identify as another gender. Our administration told them teachers couldn't tell the parents. Their testimony validated mine.

In May of that school year, we were asked to give a survey to our students. The survey would assist the administration in acknowledging teachers who had done a commendable job. That sounded like an excellent idea until I saw Survey

Question #3: "What pronoun do you prefer to identify as?" Instead of sending the survey to my students, I sent it to our Representative.

It would be inaccurate to say that what I did was easy. Instead, it was difficult, terrifying, and utterly heartbreaking. Would I lose my job? Did my administration truly believe this radical ideology?

Most of all, what would happen to our children—not only in our district but on a global scale? They were the ones Jesus died for, and weren't they given into our care and keeping? Despite everything, I confidently possessed one thing: peace. It was His peace, exceeding all understanding, just as scripture teaches. I knew that I'd acted according to my conscience and left the results in God's hands.

Miracles continued to happen! Many teachers reported similar difficulties in adapting to the district's new ideology. Transgender youth who underwent surgeries or hormone therapies traveled to the State Capitol to describe the emotional and physical harm they experienced. Senate Bill 14 *passed,* preventing hormone therapy and surgeries for transgender minors. Several people ran for our local school board, and as of November 2024, our school board became a moral majority.

Many battles have been won; however, the war remains. For example, cell phones provide instant access to pornography and allow for grooming and sex trafficking. Yet I still hear Jesus asking, "Who will go?"

Seemingly small actions, such as mentoring young people or establishing clear tech rules for kids, can make a real difference. You might be called to speak out publicly or within the church, educating others on protecting children from the enemy's harmful deceptions.

I will stand on my guard post and station myself on the rampart; And I will keep watch to see what He will speak to me and how I may reply when I am reproved.

Then the Lord answered me and said, "Record the vision and inscribe it on tablets, that the one who reads it may run. For the vision is yet for the appointed time; it hastens toward the goal, and it will not fail. Though it tarries, wait for it; for it will certainly come, it will not delay." ~ Habakkuk 2:1-3 NAS

Though it might seem like nothing's happening, Habakkuk offers a different perspective! Wait! The vision WILL come!

Reflection Questions:

Have you ever had to make a choice between following the will of man vs. the Word of God?

_____

_____

_____

How have you witnessed boldness in the face of increasing evil?

_____

_____

_____

What are the ways the Lord is leading you to rise up in your own community? Prayerfully ask the Holy Spirit for boldness and conviction.

_____

_____

_____

_____

_____

_____

One Encounter with
Jesus Christ is
Enough
to Change you,
Instantly,
Forever.
~Luis Palau~

Embrace the Encounter

DeAnna D. Cavenah

I'm very passionate about the presence of the Lord. I can live without a lot of things, but that is one thing I cannot live without nor do I ever want to. I long to have a face-to-face encounter with the Lord. I have experienced going into the presence of the Lord one way and leaving totally changed and transformed. If you can't say this about your life, it's very possible that you have never truly encountered Him. It's possible that you don't know how, and that's not to put condemnation on you. I want to help you learn how because I know the peace, joy, and beauty that comes from ascending with the Lord. It will be one of the best decisions you'll ever make in your life.

"Ascend" means to go up or climb. When you go up higher you are rising above all the activity below and you get a clearer view. To ascend the mountain of the Lord is to seek His presence with a heart yearning for deeper connection and revelation of who He is. As we embark on this spiritual journey, we are called to leave behind the distractions and weights of the world, focusing solely on encountering the Lord.

The Bible beckons us with the call to ascend: "*Who may ascend the mountain of the Lord? Who may stand in His holy place? The one who has clean hands and a pure heart, who does not trust in an idol or swear by a false god*" ~ Psalm 24:3-4. These verses remind us that to approach God, we must be pure and sincere, laying our lives bare before Him.

When we reach the summit, we find ourselves in the sacred presence of the Lord. This encounter is marked by awe and reverence, as we stand before the Creator of the universe. It is a moment of profound intimacy and revelation, where God unveils His heart and purposes to us.

In this holy place, we are invited to listen to His heart and receive. God's voice may come as a gentle whisper, a powerful declaration, or a still, small voice. Our role is to be attentive, to soak in His words, and to let them transform us.

An encounter with God naturally leads us to worship. Our response is one of adoration and gratitude, expressing our love and devotion to Him. Worship is not merely a song or a ritual; it is a lifestyle, a continuous offering of ourselves to the Lord. It's an expression that goes beyond words.

The mountain top experience is not meant to be a one-time thing but a lasting transformation. As we descend, we bring with us the revelations, the visions, and the anointing we received. Our lives become a testimony of the encounter, a demonstration of God's presence in a world in need of His light.

The encounter compels us to live differently. It challenges us to align our actions with the divine intel and revelation we have received. It empowers us to step into our calling with boldness and faith. Our journey up the mountain equips us to lead others to their own encounters with God. We become vessels of His grace, sharing the love and truth that we have discovered.

Embrace the encounter, for it is in His presence that we are truly transformed and made whole. May our lives continually reflect the glory of the mountain top and lead others to experience the same profound connection with our Heavenly Father.

Reflection Questions:

Ascending the mountain requires intentional purification. Taking time to repent and seek God's forgiveness is a crucial step in preparing for the encounter. As we reflect on our hearts, we must ask ourselves:

Are there areas of my life that hinder my walk with God or need cleansing?

_____

_____

_____

_____

How do I create space in my life to hear God's voice?

_____

_____

_____

_____

Have I ever experienced a divine encounter that left me changed?

_____

_____

_____

_____

How has that encounter influenced my daily life and decisions?

_____

_____

_____

_____

_____

Deeper Truth:
Read Psalm 27

> **Worship Encounter:**
>
> **"The Encounter"** by CT Praise
>
> **"Let My Life Be Worship"** by Bethel Music
>
> **"Encounter Song"** by Planetshakers

"I survived because the fire inside of me burns brighter than the one around me."

~Joshua Graham~

You Will Not Be Burned

Hadley Martin

"For the vision is yet for an appointed time; though it tarry, wait for it; because it will surely come." — Habakkuk 2:3

The Weight of Seeing and Sensing

Since I was young, I've experienced the world differently than most. I have sensed things before they happened, carried burdens that weren't mine, and felt the weight of what others overlooked. Being prophetic isn't just about hearing God—it's about feeling Him deeply, sometimes to the point of exhaustion. It's like holding a language that not everyone speaks, a spiritual awareness that few understand.

But it wasn't just prophetic vision—it was discernment too. I didn't just see what was happening in the spirit; I could feel the warfare behind words, the hidden wounds, the motives people tried to mask. I could sense the weight in a room before anyone spoke.

For so long, I thought I was crazy. Maybe I was overthinking. Maybe I was just too sensitive.

But I've learned that discernment and the prophetic often go hand in hand. To be prophetic is to see what God is saying. To be discerning is to sense the unseen battle behind what is happening.

And if you have both? It can feel like both a gift and a burden.

The Challenge of Seeing Beyond the Surface

One of the hardest things about carrying both prophetic vision and discernment is that it often makes you feel disconnected.

When others are comfortable with shallow conversation, you crave depth.

When others only see the present, you see the patterns, the shifts, the warfare.

When others assume everything is fine, you feel what's really happening beneath the surface.

You can walk into a room and sense the presence of something demonic before anyone else notices.

You can talk to someone and feel their battle before they admit they're struggling.

You can sit in a church service and discern the spiritual condition of the room.

It's not paranoia.
It's not overthinking.
It's discernment.

If you, like me, have these gifts, the enemy would love for you to believe that your way of seeing isolates you. But in reality, God is raising up many in this generation who carry both prophetic vision and discernment. People who aren't satisfied with empty religion. People who aren't deceived by appearances. People who can see through the fog, hear through the noise, and discern the real battle.

You are not alone in this. There are others who carry the same hunger, the same weight, the same fire. And more than anything, God Himself is with you in it.

The Warfare of Discernment and Prophetic Vision

If you are called to see, you are also called to war.

Jeremiah was a prophet, but he also wept over what others ignored (Jeremiah 9:1).

Daniel saw visions that terrified him (Daniel 7:15).

Jesus, knowing the hearts of people, often withdrew to be alone with the Father (Luke 5:16).

Because here's the reality: when you can see the war, you also feel the war.

Discernment makes you aware of what others ignore.

The prophetic makes you aware of what is coming before it arrives.

And sometimes? That feels like too much.

There were times I wished I could shut it off. Times when I sensed something dark before I even knew what it was. Times when I knew someone was battling something deep, but they weren't ready to talk about it. Times when I was burdened by something I couldn't yet explain.

But I've learned this: If God lets you see it, it's because He trusts you to pray about it.

Not everything you discern is meant to be spoken.

Not everything you sense is meant to be acted on immediately.

But everything God reveals is meant to be stewarded.

And that's why trusting His timing is everything.

Trusting the Timing of Revelation

There have been seasons when God showed me things I wasn't ready to understand—things that felt more like a burden than a blessing. I've learned that just because God reveals something now doesn't mean He's asking me to act on it now. Some visions take years to unfold.

Habakkuk 2:3 reminds us that the vision is for an appointed time. If you feel like you're carrying something too big for you, trust that God will bring clarity when the time is right. Your responsibility isn't to force the vision—it's to be faithful with what He has given you.

That might look like writing things down, praying over what you see, or simply waiting. God doesn't just give revelation; He also provides wisdom for how to steward it.

Fireproof Discernment: Why God Makes You Strong Enough to Carry It

For a long time, I thought my calling would crush me; that the weight of seeing, sensing, and discerning everything would eventually be too much. But what I didn't realize then was this: God doesn't just give the gift—He makes you strong enough to carry it.

Shadrach, Meshach, and Abednego were thrown into the fire because they refused to bow. They should have burned. They should have died. But Jesus was in the fire with them. And when they came out? They didn't even smell like smoke. (Daniel 3:27)

This calling will not consume you.
The weight of discernment will not break you.
The things you see will not destroy you.
Because Jesus is standing in it with you.
And when you walk through the fire of warfare, intercession, rejection, and carrying what others don't understand—
You will come out of it not even smelling like smoke.

You Matter, and Your Gift Matters

If you've ever felt like your gift is too much, hear me: You were built for this. God wouldn't have given you this level of discernment if He hadn't equipped you for it. He wouldn't have given you this vision if He hadn't prepared you to carry it. He wouldn't have placed this weight on you if He wasn't going to strengthen you for it.

You are not alone.
You are not crazy.
You are not too much.
You are called.
You are anointed.
You are fireproof.

And the vision is for an appointed time.

Reflection Questions:

Have you ever felt like your discernment or prophetic vision isolates you? How have you navigated that?

_____

_____

_____

In what ways has God confirmed to you that your sensitivity in the spirit is a gift, not a burden?

_____

_____

_____

How can you steward what God shows you without feeling overwhelmed?

_____

_____

_____

<u>Worship Encounter:</u>

"Spirit Lead Me" by Influence Music

"Over and Over" by Elevation Rhythm

"At The Altar" by Elevation Rhythm

"To keep a lamp
burning, we have to
keep putting
oil in it."
~Mother Teresa~

It's Time to Check My Oil

DeAnna D. Cavenah

Why do we struggle so much with our emotions? Why do we go through seasons of highs and then sink into valleys of lows?

I've always hated these seasons in my life, because I feel so inadequate, so unworthy, so incapable of becoming anything God has said I would become; so lacking to do anything He has called me to. During these times I have just wanted to isolate.

So often we get to a place where we do what we have do, yet we don't put forth the effort to do more. We lack energy and we lack zeal. It's hard to give out when we feel so empty. And then we think, '*How can I be so empty when I'm reading the Word, praying, and listening to worship music?*'

Have you ever been there? What do you do when you're doing all that you know to do, but it seems like it's just not enough?

Sometimes it could be that we are overloading ourselves with other people's demands. You can't be all things, to all people, at all times. It's okay to say no. When we are distracted and busy with other things besides that which we know to do, we are not fulfilling our callings. This can cause much confusion and uncertainty. This has become one of the enemy's greatest weapons against us. We've lost the art of being still in God's presence to actually get His heart and mind on the matter.

I'm so guilty of this very thing, and when I find myself in this place, I start to feel anxious and overwhelmed. But thank God that we can run to the Father according to Psalm 61:1-2 (AMP): "*Hear my cry, oh God; listen to my prayer. From the end of the earth I call to you, when my heart is overwhelmed and weak; lead me to the rock that is higher than I (a rock that is too high to reach without your help).*" It's a rock of safety, a refuge from our enemy, the only way to get there is with the Lord's help.

We must protect the anointing on our life, the oil that we carry. If we allow people and distractions to drain us, then we can't operate and function properly.

This reminds me of a car with an oil leak, or one where the oil has been drained completely. It will not operate correctly. The parts will grind instead of running smoothly, then seize up and stall the vehicle. The engine will be damaged and possibly ruined. The presence of oil in its distribution is absolutely crucial to the engine's continued operation.

Engines can work without oil, but the effect is so damaging that they are only capable of running for less than 30 minutes until failing, and in most cases, it's a lot quicker than that.

If a car runs out of oil, it should immediately be taken to an automotive repair shop where a professional can change the oil. If damage has occurred, he is able to identify any problems and can correct them without delay.

In the same way an oil leak can so drastically affect, damage, and shut down a car engine, so it is with our lives. To prevent leaks, we need to regularly check our engines.

I've asked the Lord a time or two, "Do I have an oil leak? Has my oil possibly drained out?"

Symptoms of an oil leak or low oil:
#1- The warning light comes on (check engine)
#2- You leave oil stains wherever you are parked
#3- The engine begins to knock
#4- There is a burning smell
#5- It doesn't matter how much you put in, it drains out
#6- Smoke comes from the front of the engine
#7- The engine starts to overheat
#8- You start spending more on fuel

Damage from driving with low oil:
#1- The valves start to burn up
#2- The seals dry out

#3- The internal parts heat up and eventually deform and break. Until something breaks, the engine will continue to lose power and burn more fuel while running poorly.

Just as regular and scheduled check-ups are necessary and vital to a car engine, so it is with our heart life. Let's not ignore the warning signs. It's very possible that we need to run to the master mechanic, Jesus, without delay.

When our oil gets changed, so does the filter. We must filter our life through the Word of God and allow it to cleanse and purify us from all impurities.

I Samuel 16:1 - *Now the Lord said to Samuel, "You have mourned long enough for Saul. I have rejected him as king of Israel, so fill your flask with olive oil and go to Bethlehem. Find a man named Jesse who lives there, for I have selected one of his sons to be my king."*

The oil is so important. Whenever oil is absent in the presence of movement, you have friction. You can lose a lot of things but don't lose your oil.

Get ready for an oil change. Nothing the enemy throws at you will be able to stick because of the oil.

Isaiah 54:17 - *But I promise you, no weapon meant to hurt you will succeed, and you will refute every accusing word spoken against you.*

Today if you feel like you have an oil leak, here are some thoughts to ponder:

- ❖ Being in the wrong lane can drain you of your oil.
- ❖ Doing things the Lord hasn't called you to do will drain your oil.
- ❖ Saying yes to everything and everyone will drain your oil.
- ❖ When you don't spend time in prayer or in His word your oil will drain out.
- ❖ Disobedience will drain your oil.
- ❖ A bad or negative attitude can drain your oil.
- ❖ Competition and comparison can drain your oil.

Reflection Questions:

1. Are there areas in my life where I am operating outside of what the Lord has called me to do?

_____

_____

_____

2. Am I overwhelming myself by saying "yes" to too many commitments, leaving little or no time in the presence of the Lord or reading His word?

_____

_____

_____

3. Have I been ignoring the warning signs that I have a spiritual oil leak? If yes, how can I cultivate a more positive and obedient mindset to maintain the flow of my spiritual oil without unnecessary leaks?

_____

_____

_____

_____

_____

4. What are some specific ways that I can protect and sustain the oil I carry?

_____

_____

_____

_____

_____

Dig Deeper:
Matthew 25:1-13 (the Parable of Ten Virgins)
Psalm 23:5
2 Kings 4:1-7

<u>Worship Encounter:</u>

"Oil in My Lamp" by UpperRoom Prayer Set

"Fill Me Up/All My Oil Medley"

by Bruna Olmeda

"Fresh Oil" by New Wine

If following Christ
has never cost you
anything, you're not
following Him.
~Tim Conway~

The Cost of Following Jesus

Izabel Buxton

I vividly remember the day I called off my engagement. It was a Sunday morning, and I woke up knowing that "today had to be the day I made up my mind once and for all." Sitting in church next to my youth group, I had an overwhelming realization—this wasn't the life I wanted to live, nor was it the example I wanted to set. I was lost in a cloud of confusion, struggling to see past my own plans and to see God's instead.

Just days before, I had met with my mentor, who pulled the gold out of me, spoke truth in love, and reminded me of a simple truth: I am made for Him. That meeting was a turning point. Was the decision easy? No. But was it worth it? Absolutely.

Having a mentor in my life at that moment was crucial. A mentor is someone who sees things from a perspective you might not be able to, especially when emotions cloud your judgment. My mentor didn't just listen to my struggles; she spoke truth to me with love and compassion. She didn't tell me what I wanted to hear but what I needed to hear: that God had something better for me, something that would align with His purpose for my life. Her words were like a light in the darkness, guiding me toward obedience, even when I wasn't sure where that obedience would lead.

Two years earlier, before I left for ministry school, my mentor asked to meet with me. I was a bit nervous, but excited that she, my pastor, would take time to speak wisdom into my life before I left for a life-changing journey. During that meeting, she shared a passage from Luke 14:25-35, and I want to share some of it with you:

"As massive crowds followed Jesus, He turned to them and said, 'When you follow me as my disciple, you must put aside your father, your mother, your wife, your sisters, your brothers; it will even seem as though you hate your own life. This is the price you'll pay to be considered one of my followers. Anyone who comes to me must be willing to share my cross and experience it as his own, or he cannot be considered my disciple... unless you surrender all to me, giving up all you possess, you cannot be one of my disciples."

At that time, I didn't know what the future held. Trusting God for finances, losing friends, believing for restoration in my family, and experiencing inner healing—all of these came after that meeting, along with the difficult decision to end my engagement. But through it all, this scripture became my lifeline.

I had to make a choice; I was willing to pay the cost. The decision wasn't easy, but I said yes to it. I realized my life isn't my own, but His. The call to follow Jesus is weighty, requiring sacrifice, but it's also filled with hope. Reflecting on these past two years since calling off my engagement and graduating from ministry school, I can honestly say it was worth it.

Since then, all finances for my school have been covered, my relationship with my mom is restored, and I've learned who I am as a daughter of the King more than ever before.

There were countless moments when I felt alone, misunderstood, or discouraged. But in those moments, I found a deeper connection to Jesus. His story became mine, and I realized that my story wasn't just for me—it was for the people around me. The fruit of our lives, the sacrifices we make, and the costs we pay aren't just for our benefit; they impact the spheres of influence around us.

Perhaps you're reading this and asking, "What's the point of all this?" The point is this: there is hope. In the sacrifice, in the pain, in the pressing, there is oil. And that oil is a sweet aroma to God. It is beautiful to Him. You are not defined by what you've been through. You are not your past. But God will use your story, your experiences, and your obedience to bring glory to His name.

The day I called off my engagement there was a train graffitied with the word "Hope"; that stayed there for six months and I truly believe it was my sign from God: that He is hope.

Had I not been obedient in calling off my engagement, so many things would not have happened. What doors would have opened from closing another? You never know what lies behind your "yes," or your "no." The cost may be high but will forever be worth it.

Reflection Questions:

Is there someone in your life who can speak truth in love to you, especially in moments of confusion or struggle?

_____

How can you cultivate that relationship and be open to receiving their guidance?

_____

_____

What are some areas in your life where you feel God is calling you to surrender or sacrifice?

_____

_____

What might be standing in the way of fully saying "yes" to Him?

_____

_____

What does the cost of following Jesus look like in your life?

_____

_____

Are you willing to surrender all for Him?

_____

Jesus Calls Us to Recapture Childlike FAITH; A faith that is open to moments of awe and WONDER.

~Unknown~

Child-Like Trust

DeAnna D. Cavenah

One day some parents brought their children to Jesus so he could touch and bless them. But the disciples scolded the parents for bothering him. When Jesus saw what was happening, he was angry with his disciples. He said to them, "Let the children come to me. Don't stop them! For the Kingdom of God belongs to those who are like these children. I tell you the truth, anyone who doesn't receive the Kingdom of God like a child will never enter it." Then he took the children in his arms and placed his hands on their heads and blessed them. ~ Mark 10:13-16 NLT

Why do we make trusting God so hard? He wants us to come to Him just like a little child. When I tell my son Ethan, who is now 17 years old, something, though he is not so much a little child anymore, he trusts me and believes what I tell him. He'll often remind me of things I've said, and he holds me to my word.

How much more can we trust God and hold Him to His Word? He is the One who gave it all for us: His only Son to die for us and be raised back to life, giving us the Hope of Eternal Life! Not only that, but He left behind the Blueprint to build our life upon: His Word! We can hold God to His Word.

Everything we need is in His Word. It is our final authority. Today, go to God with childlike faith; trust His word with simplicity and receptivity. He wants you to know and understand that You Matter to Him.

Deeper Truth:
Matthew 18:3
Proverbs 3:5-6 (AMP)

Reflection Questions:

In what areas of your life do you find it hardest to trust God with the simplicity and confidence of a child, and why?

_____

_____

_____

_____

_____

_____

_____

How can you remind yourself daily to rely on God's Word as the blueprint for your decisions and actions, holding Him to His promises?

_____

_____

_____

_____

_____

_____

_____

Reflect on a time when you experienced God's faithfulness by trusting Him like a child. How did that experience strengthen your faith and trust in Him?

_____

_____

_____

_____

_____

_____

_____

_____

_____

_____

Worship Encounter:

"I Trust Jesus" by Matthew West and Jenn Johnson

"I Believe" by Charity Gayle

"I Will Trust" by Red Rocks Worship

As we trust God when it doesn't make sense, He is good beyond what we can imagine. ~Kristen Miller~

The Trust Challenge

Denise LeDoux Leiato

As I look back on my life, I marvel at the good things God has done for me. The word says in James 1:17, "Every good and perfect gift is from above and comes down from the father of lights with whom there is no variation or shadow of turning."

Although I have been through deaths, divorce, and disease, I can still declare the goodness of God. He has taken the bad and good and woven those threads into a beautiful tapestry because I matter to him and so do you! He will do the same for you because He is no respecter of persons. I've had highs and lows in my life, yet He was always there. Hebrews 13:5 says, "I will never leave or forsake you." What a wonderful promise for us, if only we trust Him.

Genesis 1:28 says, "Be fruitful and multiply," yet how was I to do that? I wondered at one point in my life. After taking chemo for breast cancer, I was told my eggs could be damaged and if I got pregnant, I could have a child with severe disabilities. Being a special education teacher, I knew that could be devastating, so my husband and I took extra precautions. Yet one night we threw caution to the wind, and I became pregnant.

Let me digress for a moment. I had been married before and lost a baby prematurely due to an incompetent cervix, one that thinned out so much it could not hold the pregnancy. I started having premature contractions, which resulted in too early of a delivery. My baby, Anna Maria, had lungs that were not fully developed so she transitioned to heaven without much of a life experience here on earth. She had only a few hours before she was in the arms of Jesus.

So here I was pregnant for a second time with my new husband, George. I had a blood test to validate the pregnancy assumption and made an appointment with my gynecologist/obstetrician. After examining me, he proceeded to fuss at me for getting pregnant, telling me it was dangerous as the breast cancer I had experienced previously was estrogen-positive. Estrogen levels increase during pregnancy, so he was very solemn and not encouraging. I realized he probably had my best interest at heart, but he did not show that, so I left his office in tears.

I drove straight to church where the secretary connected me with another church member. Linda knew of a great doctor who would possibly take my case. Although he was not delivering babies anymore, he agreed to take me since he liked a challenge. And boy, was I a challenge!

I started bleeding at the same time a hurricane was headed in our direction. The doctor told me I could come in for a sonogram after the storm passed, but I impatiently asked if I could go in that day. Of course, the kind doctor agreed, so I found out the pregnancy was viable. I was put on bed rest with the promise that when I was further along, I would have a procedure to close my cervix to protect the baby. It was called a cerclage. I was told I would be able to return to teaching after the surgery.

The surgery was done as promised, and I returned to teaching around September, but one Saturday as my husband and father were on a trail ride, I began to experience Braxton Hicks contractions, or false labor. It was too early in the pregnancy for these to be happening. So nervously, I drove myself to the hospital several blocks away. I lay in the hospital bed with my Bible beside me. When I opened it, 2 Kings 4:16 was on the page. It read, "Next year at this time you will have a son." That was God's word to me in that moment; I was going to carry my baby and not lose him. I returned home, full of hope, with a promise from God. This passage illustrates not just a miraculous gift, but a profound assurance of God's attentiveness to our needs.

At that time, my doctor was checking me weekly . After the hospital visit, he sent me to a specialist near New Orleans. His report was not encouraging; he gave me a 50-50 chance of making it to Christmas. The baby was due in March.

My father took me to the doctor's appointment because George could not miss work for two days. My father and I spent the night at a motel before embarking on the drive home since it was a long drive. As I lay in the motel room in my twin bed with tears filling my eyes, I vowed to the Lord that I would tell everyone about this child if He would just let me have him!

After traveling home, I was given medication, a monitor to measure contractions, and was told to stay in bed. I wasn't even supposed to go to my weekly doctor appointments. To help accomplish the goal of staying in bed, church members took turns coming to our house and preparing lunch for me. I wore the monitor around my middle and "called in" to a special number. If contractions showed up on the monitor, I was told to drink a pitcher of water and then monitor and call back again. I did this daily, three times a day.

My friend, Edie, brought her two young sons who sat at the end of my bed while she cleaned my bathroom. My childhood dance friend, Mary, let me borrow her father's bedside commode so I would not have to make trips down the long hall to empty my bladder. Staying hydrated to prevent contractions helped fill up that bedside commode, which my dedicated husband emptied every day when he returned home from work. We truly were all working to bring this child into the world!

I wish I could say I read my Bible all day and listened to praise music, but honestly, I was very anxious, and monitoring my womb took up a lot of my time and emotional energy. It felt like I was holding my breath and jumping from a cliff daily; I just had to trust the Lord. I had gotten that promise from him in the hospital. Wasn't that enough? It should have been, but the battle was in my mind. The enemy of my soul tried to put fear in me. I just had to do what Proverbs 3:5 says: "Trust in the Lord with all your heart and do not rely on your own opinions."

Trust means belief in the reliability, ability or strength of something or someone. In the Old Testament, trusting faith was a Hebrew word that meant a rope, providing security, tying you to someone you could depend on. I did lean heavily upon and trust in the Lord. I was not only holding onto that rope; I felt like I was holding on by a thread. It was only His grace that carried me through. I had seen what God had done in my life, bringing me through breast cancer, bringing a godly man to be my husband, and I trusted that he would do a miracle again. Jesus does not change. "Jesus Christ is the same yesterday and today and forever." Hebrews 13:8

So, as time went on, I remembered my doctor was going to leave town in late February for the Washington DC Mardi Gras Ball. Since my delivery date was sometime in March, I discussed it with the doctor. Who would deliver the baby in his absence if I went into labor? I did not want some "stranger" delivering my baby after all I had been through. The doctor then suggested an x-ray of the baby be taken, and if the bones of his knees were developed, it was safe for me to deliver. We got the x-ray and learned it was safe, so we made plans for a Valentine's Day delivery—a very special delivery!

I quit taking my medication to stop labor, but nothing happened. I had to be induced on Wednesday, February 14, 1990. After having an epidural and delivering a beautiful, blonde baby boy, I almost hemorrhaged to death. Thank goodness George was still with me after we greeted our son! George began praying in his prayer language, a heavenly tongue, as I felt the life going out of me, but I recovered and eventually was given a blood transfusion. Days later, I was finally released to go home with our precious promised child.

That was 35 years ago. My son and his wife had their first child and made us grandparents. God is so faithful! If only we put trust in Him and His word, we can please Him.

"Without faith, it is impossible to please God." Hebrews 11:6

My friend, look back at the things that God has done for you. Then trust in him, no matter the circumstance.

Romans 8:38 in The Passion Translation says, "So we are convinced that every detail of our lives is woven together for good, for we are his lovers who have been called to fulfill his designed purpose." God works all things for good for those who love him; realize that God is weaving a tapestry with the circumstances of your life. It will be beautiful and bring glory to Him.

Genesis. 50:20 says, "you meant evil against me, but God meant yet for good.". He can turn things around because He loves us and has a purpose for us.

Deeper Truth:
Psalm 37:5: "Commit your way to the Lord; trust in him, and he will act."
Isaiah 41:10: "Fear not, for I am with you; be not dismayed, for I am your God; I will strengthen you. I will help you; I will uphold you with my righteous hand."
Jeremiah 17:7: "Blessed is the man who trusts in the Lord, whose trust is the Lord."

As you focus on trust in the Lord, I leave you with this:

T-R-U-S-T
T is for TRULY
R is for REVEALING
U is for TO US
S is for THE SAVIOR'S
T is for TENDER CARE

Trust truly reveals to us the Savior's tender care!

Jesus has overcome and so shall we if we trust in Him!

Reflection Questions:

Consider the TRUST acronym given. How have you experienced this in your life?

_____

_____

_____

_____

_____

Have you struggled to trust the Lord? Reflect on a time in your life that required trust to navigate. What was the outcome?

_____

_____

_____

_____

_____

What is one step you can take to choose to TRUST Him moving forward?

_____

_____

_____

Worship Encounter:

"Trust in God" by Elevation Worship

"Promises" by Maverick City Music

"You're Gonna Be Ok" Johnson by Brian and Jenn Johnson

"Goodness of God" by Bethel Music

Holding a grudge
doesn't make you
strong;
it makes you bitter.
Forgiving doesn't
make you weak;
it sets you free.
~Dave Willis~

Forgiveness

Melissa Richard

It started out like any other day. I was at work, and I stayed in for lunch to listen to a teaching by Charles Stanley on forgiveness. It was so powerful, and it forever changed my life.

My husband had walked out on me about a month before I heard this teaching. I had started to suspect there might be another woman. The day after hearing the teaching, I got a call at work which confirmed my suspicions. He *had* been seeing another woman. I did not expect it to hit me the way it did. It was as if someone had stabbed me in the heart. I thought I didn't care anymore. My feelings had been shoved down so deeply; but they all came out that day. I was in shock. How could he have done this to me? The betrayal hit me like a ton of bricks.

A couple of days went by, and he drove up to the house to get something. I had a chance to put into practice everything that I had heard about forgiveness. It was not pretty, but I did it! I said, "I forgive you and I forgive her! I refuse to let you steal my joy and my peace!"

Like I said, it wasn't pretty or perfect, but I forgave them! I made a decision that day and had to make it every day for months until it finally started to get easier. Every time I thought about it, I would say, "I forgive." It was hard, but it was so worth it.

I didn't feel anything at first, but after a couple of months, my heart started to heal. When I saw him, it didn't hurt so much. And before I knew it, the feelings of anger, resentment and pain were gone! God had healed my broken heart. If He did it for me, He can do it for you.

It all starts by making a choice. When you say you forgive, it's not saying what the other person did was okay. It's about making a choice to not allow what was done to you make you into a bitter and angry person. With the help of the Holy Spirit, you can forgive. I'll say it again: if He did it for me, He can do it for you! Don't allow that hurt and pain to turn you into a bitter, angry person. Choose to forgive and be free.

Reflection Questions:

Is there someone that I need to forgive today?

_____

How has holding onto past hurts and grievances affected my emotional and spiritual well-being?

_____

_____

_____

What steps can I take today to begin the process of forgiveness, and how might this decision impact my future relationships and personal peace?

_____

_____

_____

Worship Encounter:
"You Can" by Hope Darst
"Forgiveness" by Matthew West
"God Help Me" by Unspoken

The Three-Word Prayer God Loves: CHANGE ME, LORD.

~Stormie Omartian~

Lord, I'm Angry!

DeAnna D. Cavenah

Have you ever found yourself angry with a person, but could not pinpoint why that person was getting under your skin? Sister, surely, I can't be the only one. Ok, so for all the real folks, let's talk!

According to psychology, anger is a byproduct of fear and rejection. We may use anger as a defense mechanism when feeling vulnerable or threatened by perceived rejection, essentially using anger as a way to cope with underlying feelings of fear and insecurity; this is especially true when experiencing social rejection.

So here are some key points to consider:

#1- Anger is linked to the "fight" response in our bodies' stress response, which can be triggered by feelings of fear or threat, including perceived rejection.

#2- Anger is often considered a secondary emotion, meaning it can arise as a reaction to primary emotions like fear, sadness, or frustration.

#3- When someone feels rejected, anger can act as a way to protect oneself by expressing aggression or asserting dominance.

Do any of these key points resonate with you? I think we could take it to another key point called Jealousy. If I could insert an emoji right here, it would be the one with the hand over the face with one eye looking through the fingers. No one likes to admit it, but that is a major root for anger.

The Bible says that jealousy is as cruel as the grave. We don't like to even admit that it could be the root issue. Well, let's go ahead and deal with it and speak some truth into your situation.

Truth #1- No one can take away what God has placed in or on you.

Truth #2- No one has the power to make you feel inferior unless you give them permission.

Truth #3- You were born for greatness!

I could have given you many more truths, but I think you get the point.

So let's deal with the root of this thing and not only cut it out but destroy it. The Word says you are the salt of the earth! Salt is a method used to completely destroy roots! As the salt of the earth, with the help of Holy Spirit dwelling within you, you have the power to demolish and destroy every root of rejection, fear, bitterness, resentment, anger, and jealousy! These are all roots of sin, and we need to develop a new root system from a Heavenly Biblical perspective.

Colossians 2:7 says, "*Let your roots grow down into Him, and let your lives be built on Him. Then your faith will grow strong in the truth you were taught, and you will overflow with thankfulness.*"

Jeremiah 17:7-10 (AMP) says, "*Blessed (with spiritual security) is the man who believes and trusts in and relies on the Lord and whose hope and confident expectation is the Lord. For he will be nourished like a tree planted by the waters, that spreads out its roots by the river; and will not fear the heat when it comes; but its leaves will be green and moist. And it will not be anxious and concerned in a year of drought nor stop bearing fruit. The heart is deceitful above all things and it is extremely sick; who can understand it fully and know its secret motives? I, the Lord, search and examine the mind, I test the heart, to give to each man according to his ways, according to the results of his deeds.*"

Jesus is very serious about our root system and the soil of our hearts. He says in Mark 7:20, "It is what comes from inside of us that defiles us."

Today allow Holy Spirit to shine His light into the soil of your heart and dig out any roots of anger, fear, insecurity, or jealousy. Let His Spirit renew your thoughts and attitudes so that you can take on the nature of God who is truly righteous and holy.

Deeper Truth:
Matthew 5:13 (NLT)
Matthew 13:15-17 (NLT)
Song of Songs 8:6 (NLT)

Reflection Questions:

Are there any roots of anger, rejection, fear, bitterness, resentment, or jealousy that I need to identify and uproot from my heart?

_____

_____

How can I allow Holy Spirit to examine the soil of my heart and reveal any hidden motives or unhealthy roots that need to be addressed and healed?

_____

_____

In what ways can I cultivate a new root system based on a Heavenly Biblical perspective, as described in Colossians 2:7 and Jeremiah 17:7-10, to grow in spiritual security and bear good fruit?

_____

_____

Worship Encounter:
"You Won't Relent"
by Jesus Culture
"This is My Desire" by Hillsong
"Change Me" Tamela Mann

For the WEAPONS of OUR warfare are not carnal, but MIGHTY through GOD to the pulling down of STRONGHOLDS, casting down arguments and every high thing that exalts itself against the knowledge of God, bringing every thought into captivity to the obedience of Christ.
~II Corinthians 10:4-5~

Take Your Position

Poem by DeAnna D. Cavenah

I didn't want to get out of bed;
There were too many voices in my head.
I didn't want to face another day,
But I knew I needed to get up and pray.

As I lay there the choice was mine to make
If I chose to pull the covers up, my soul would be at stake.
I knew the enemy wanted me to go back in a shell
Of that I would call, "a self-made hell."

I tried to dismiss the battle going on
So, I chose a distraction and picked up my phone.
To my mind it seemed like an easy fix,
But the battle between flesh and spirit just didn't mix.

As the voice of the Spirit became louder in my head
I knew I could no longer lay in that bed.
So, as I started my morning routine
A new freshness to my life the Lord would bring.

As I sat with tears running down my face
I knew I made the right choice because He met me in that place.
As I began to pour out my heart
His goodness, loving-kindness, and mercy offered me a brand-
new start.

You'll always have these two choices, you see,
But there is only one that brings you true victory.
So before you choose to roll over and play dead,
Remember that you are not the tail, Christ has made you the
head.

In Christ, you have all authority
So don't for a minute give in to the plan of the enemy.
He says, "Take Your Position" in the secret place with Me,
And in My presence, you'll have joy, peace, and that called true
liberty.

You Truly Matter and that is a fact
So keep your eyes on Me and don't look back.
Who the Son sets free is free indeed;
Stay close to me, for I'm all you need.

Tucked away in the piney woods of Reeves, LA, you will find Lighthouse Ministries a child residential facility especially designed for young unwed pregnant girls and their children. The lighthouse gives a greater opportunity for success and a safe place that enables these young teen moms to live and care for their babies until they reach 18. The lighthouse offers a wide range of services and classes including: homeschool, life and job skills, anger management, childbirth and newborn care, breast-feeding, infant CPR, Bible study, cooking, etiquette, sewing, crafts, social events, root causes of addictions, and one on one counseling. We have a full staff and qualified volunteers who assist in the healing and education of these girls on a daily basis.

Through experience, we have learned that God has not equipped the government to set the captives free, but as Luke 4:18 states, "He has called us as Christians to heal the brokenhearted and proclaim liberty to the captives."

Our mission statement is "For I know the plans I have for you, declares the Lord. Plans to prosper you and not to harm you, plans to give you hope and a future." - Jeremiah 29:11

We are a nonprofit 501 C-3 organization supported by monthly partners.

To learn more about Lighthouse Ministries and how you can partner with us visit:

www.lighthouseministriesinc.org
or Email: Admin@lighthouseministriesinc.org

About DeAnna

DeAnna Cavenah is a wife, mom, grandmother, Speaker, Published Author of "Not Defined by the Struggle," Worship Pastor and Songwriter, but most importantly, a Lover of Jesus Christ.

She graduated in 1989 from Delta School of Business in Lake Charles, LA with a Business Degree in Word Processing Technology. She pursued her career as an Office Manager for many years before she ventured out to become a Real Estate Agent and later became the owner of her own business, The Treasure Chest.

She also served as Household Manager for Lighthouse Ministries, Inc., a Home for Unwed Mothers located in Reeves, LA for many years until the Lord called her into full-time ministry. She is a 2021 Graduate from Eagles International Training Institute of Dallas, TX in School of Worship. She is also a 2022 Graduate of EITI from the School of The Authors.

She passionately pursues the call of God on her life and is dedicated to imparting the same fire and passion she carries on to others. DeAnna serves in many areas of ministry but is most passionate about leading women into a life of wholeness with a message of hope, healing, and restoration. DeAnna understands the power of the Redemptive work of the cross after needing much healing and deliverance herself from addictive behaviors, suicidal attempts, rejection, betrayal, and brokenness. She believes that we become whole when we embrace the truth that our identity is in Christ alone. As a Worship Pastor and Songwriter, she has the privilege to not only lead her own congregation into the presence of the Lord each week, but has had the opportunity to minister in many other countries such as South Africa, Peru, Grenada, and Belize.

DeAnna Co-Pastors Full Life Assembly of God in Dequincy, Louisiana alongside of her husband Greg of 35 years at the time of this book. Pastors Greg and DeAnna reside in Reeves, Louisiana. They have two sons, Michael Scott, Ethan Grant and one granddaughter, Rosaleigh.

Learn more and connect with DeAnna at:

www.dequincyfulllife.com
Email: *Passionate4Praise@yahoo.com*

To connect further with any of the authors from this devotional, reach out to DeAnna and request more information.

Sometimes we go through seasons of brokenness and uncertainty that seem to last forever and we wonder if it will ever change.

Whatever season of life you find yourself in today, know that you are not defined by the struggle, you are stronger. There is beauty to be found and lessons to be learned as you lean in and embrace each season of your life.

Through this 40 Day Devotion you will realize that nothing is wasted. As you embrace an encounter with the Lord, He will take you deeper into His heart. He is wanting to take you on a journey to experience a life full of passion and purpose.

Purchase your copy at: amazon.com/dp/B0CJHTT6TZ

Part of life is experiencing difficult things. There are seasons of joy and seasons of pain. But it's important to remember that these are just that... seasons. They won't last forever. More importantly, you are never alone. God is with you. He sees you. He will carry you through. And He always makes the broken beautiful and uses everything for good.

It's so easy to slip into despair, worry, fear, hopelessness... But God has grace that abounds beyond what you can imagine. And part of rising out of that is through others' testimonies.

That's exactly what you'll find in *She Laughs at the Future*.

This collection of testimonies shares real stories from those who went through some of life's most difficult challenges and yet came out with faith and hope and strength greater than ever. Renew your faith and walk in the joy and peace that allows you to *laugh without fear of the future*.

Get your copy of She Laughs at the Future
wherever books are sold.

Thank You!

Thank you so much for reading. We hope you have been inspired and encouraged by these stories. If you were touched, would you share your honest review on the book page? It will help us reach more readers and impact more lives.

Then, will you also share with someone you know?

We appreciate you!